IN THIS ISSUE

THE APOCALYPSE

Lucky Peach

EDITOR-IN-CHIEF
Chris Ying

EDITORS
Peter Meehan & David Chang

MANAGING EDITOR
Rachel Khong

ART DIRECTOR
Walter Green

CONTRIBUTING EDITOR
Eli Horowitz

CHIEF FILM CRITIC
Anthony Bourdain

FISH MURDERER
Jonathan Heindemause

ITALIAN PHOTOGRAPHER & MALE HAND MODEL
Gabriele Stabile & Mark Ibold

DISTRIBUTION & BUSINESS
Adam Krefman & Laura Howard

PEOPLE WE'D WELCOME IN OUR FALLOUT SHELTER
Johan Agrell, Jordan Bass, Sukey Bernard, Massimo Bottura, Molly Bradley, Tonya Brock, Chloe Brownstein, Sue Chan, Ira Chute, Christine Ciszczon, Hannah Clark, Brian Close, Wylie Dufresne, Rachel Dutton, Dan Felder, Jordan Frosolone, Lara Gilmore, Will Georgantas, Ryan Healey, Hidden Villa (and their lovely cow, Cleo), Chelsea Hogue, Ami Hovstadius, Greg Iwaniec, Kathryn Johnson, Per-Anders Jorgensen, Benjamin Khong, Genevieve Ko, Mattias Kroon, Marissa Louise, Jeremy Lundborg, Vanessa Martini, Dan McKinley, Brian McMullen (for consulting on the cover design of LP5), Malin Nyberg, Naoki O'Bryan, Alex Pemoulie, Josh Plunkett, Marie Elizabeth Porter, Russell Quinn, Lisa Randall, Bill Rankin, Sam Riley, Genevieve Roth, Drew Salmon, Bob Schultz, Marc Sidel, Pat Sims, Peter Smith, Sarah St. Lifer, Aaron Thier, Sunra Thompson, Justin Tripp, Ursula Viglietta, Enrico Vignoli, Rob Willey, Daniel Wikey, Jami Witek, Kim Witherspoon, Laurie Woolever, Nina Yoh, and the entire McSweeney's and Momofuku families

ADDITIONAL THANKS
To the fine people at Visit Sweden and Dark Rye (*darkrye.com*) for helping bring the Frankenchicken to life (*see page 116*). Also, the transgressive fine-art photographer Jill Greenberg, whose photographs inspired (and accompany) the story "Last Supper." The photos are part of an exhibition called Commentary and Dissent. The scenes in the photographs all occurred as photographed.

PRESS INQUIRIES
Alyson Sinclair, alyson@mcsweeneys.net | Sue Chan, press@momofuku.com

CUSTOMER SERVICE
helpme@lky.ph

FRONT-COVER PHOTO BY SARA CWYNAR
INSIDE-FRONT, INSIDE-BACK, AND BACK COVER COLLAGES BY BETH HOECKEL

LOGOTYPE BY BRIAN McMULLEN

© Copyright 2013 *Lucky Peach* and the individual contributors.

by Allen Yuen

McSWEENEY'S
SAN FRANCISCO

Lucky Peach is published quarterly in November, February, May, and August by McSweeney's Publishing LP, 849 Valencia Street, San Francisco, CA 94110. Periodicals postage pending San Francisco, CA and additional mailing offices. POSTMASTER: Send address changes to Lucky Peach, 849 Valencia Street, San Francisco, CA 94110-1737. Printed in St. Cloud, MN by Quad/Graphics.

Subscriptions: *store.mcsweeneys.net*
Lucky Peach online at: *lky.ph* Twitter: @luckypeach

THE APOCALYPSE ISSUE

One day I went to Chang's office to do something—perhaps to plan the next issue of this magazine?—and I found him in an agitated state, talking the ears off of a roomful of people who were trying in earnest to get some work done. He asked me if I'd seen *Collapse*. I hadn't. "Let's watch it now!" he proposed/insisted.

Being no great fan of ever doing anything, I put aside whatever the day's tasks were and huddled with Dave around his iPad, watching *Collapse* on Netflix. It's an exposé as interrogation, a feature-length interview with Michael C. Ruppert, a reporter, who chronicles how our current economic and energy systems will systematically fail, and how our civilization will collapse soon after. Usually Chang's urgent-urgent-watch-me-now movie recommendations are ESPN documentaries. This one was different. He was riled. He thought this guy was *right*. He was possessed by the idea that collapse was imminent. And while the rest of us had our hearts set on a more sunset-and-fishing-poles theme for this issue, I saw what was actually in store: an issue of *Lucky Peach* dedicated to the Apocalypse.

That is what you hold in your hands. We have cleaved it into two parts: the first half is pre-apocalyptic. It's about preparation for whatever form The End Times take. Then there's a swell of rapturous art in the middle. That signals the start of the second half, the part beyond Thunderdome: the time after the fall, when the zombies and robots and werebeavers have taken over. But I don't want to spoil the disgusting fun of it all. Dig in herewith, can-opener near at hand, torch at the ready.

—PETER MEEHAN

The End of the World as We Know It

Why reimagining the way we live is the only way we'll survive | **An Interview with Michael Pollan**

Is the way we're eating going to lead to the end of the world?

The way we eat now is having a profound effect on climate change, which certainly threatens to bring about the end of the world as we've known it.

For better and worse, the industrial food system has made food very cheap, and the poor can eat a better diet than they once could. It used to be that only the rich could eat meat every day of the week. Now just about everyone can, three meals a day. Fast-food chains make it easy. It's not very good meat, and most of it is brutally produced, but it is within reach.

But meat has a tremendous carbon footprint: beef in particular, because it takes so much grain to get a pound of beef. It takes about fifteen pounds of grain to get one pound of beef, and that grain takes tremendous amounts of fossil fuel—in the form of fertilizer, pesticide, farm equipment, processing, and transportation. All told, it takes fifty-five calories of fossil-fuel energy to get one calorie of beef. The average for processed foods is ten calories of fossil fuel per calorie of food.

Before World War II, every calorie of fossil-fuel energy put into a farm—in the form of diesel energy for tractors, and in fertilizer—yielded 2.3 calories of food. That's nature's free lunch—the difference between that one calorie in and the 2.3 out, which is the result of solar energy. Now it takes ten calories of fossil-fuel chain to produce a single calorie of food. It's absurd that we're now running an energy deficit with food, the production of which is theoretically based on photosynthesis. It should be the one area in our lives that is carbon neutral or even better, because plants are really the only way to take energy from the sun.

Our goal should be to eat from the solar food chain to the extent we can and not from the fossil-fuel chain, which is what we're mainly doing now. The question becomes: how do you do that? We have some powerful models. Grass-fed beef is basically a system where the sun feeds the grass, the grass feeds the ruminants, and the ruminants feed us. You're eating sunlight when you eat from that food chain. Resolarizing the food chain should be our goal in every way—taking advantage of the everyday miracle that is photosynthesis.

We're not doing that, because fossil fuel's been so cheap. Over time, farms have been substituting fossil fuel for human labor as well as the energy of the sun. Fertilizer made with natural gas or diesel was a huge step away from using the sun. It is only in the last few years that people are starting to realize the role food can play in fixing environmental problems, and the fact that we're not going to tackle global warming without reforming the food system.

Take, for example, Assembly Bill 32 in California. The law is designed to gradually bring down the amount of carbon emitted by our fuel companies, power companies, and our cars by capping carbon emissions. But the law doesn't deal with agriculture. They didn't know how to deal with agriculture, so they simply left it out. But by not capping agriculture, the state will be playing Whac-a-Mole. As all these other industries' outputs go down, agriculture's will continue to go up. We have to learn to deal with the effects of agricultural practices—especially cattle feedlots—or we're never going to get a handle on carbon. We shouldn't have as much dairy in California as we do—it's that simple. It's a desert, and cows need grass. Relocalizing food economies can—not necessarily will, but can—help reduce our reliance on fossil fuel.

What can we do on an individual level?

Home cooking is very important to solving these environmental issues. As long as we're letting big corporations cook for us, we will have an industrialized agriculture that is too big and too abusive of resources. When McDonald's or KFC is doing the cooking, they'll buy their ingredients from the biggest producers possible. They want to go to one company for all their potatoes, one company for all their beef. Big deals best with big. They understand one another. That

Interview by Rachel Khong
Photos by Dark Igloo
Cookies by Sugarbuilt

way they can achieve economies of scale and have the lowest "transaction costs"—the fewest contracts and negotiations. If you get all your beef from one meat packer, it's one contract, but if you buy from five hundred ranchers you need five hundred contracts, that many more lawyers, and that much more paperwork.

At a certain point the national movement toward a more sustainable food system will come to a halt if people don't cook. The farmers' market movement is limited by people's willingness to cook. If cooking continues to decline, there is no hope of building an alternative agriculture.

When did home cooking begin to decline in this country?

After World War II. I've spent a lot of time trying to understand that story. The usual version is that women went to work and didn't have time to cook anymore. The feminist argument—a reasonable one—was that cooking—along with other forms of housework—is oppressive.

But the more I looked at that story, the more complicated it seemed. I think what was happening when women went to work and the second wave of feminism arrived was that a lot of tension developed between men and women around housework. If women were going to work and bring in a second income, there had to be a renegotiation of the division of labor at home. There was cleaning, there was child care, there was cooking. People who could afford to outsourced their cleaning and their child care, in a sense, by hiring nannies and babysitters. But women felt differently about cooking than they did about other kinds of housework. They liked cooking. They saw cooking as part of child care and one of the enjoyable parts of being at home. Especially when cooking was not done in isolation. A lot of sociologists have asked women to rate different domestic activities— what they like best—and cooking ranks quite high. But there was no longer enough time to do it, and they needed men to step forward to help. But before that difficult conversation could be completed, before that negotiation could be wrapped up, the food industry stepped in and said, "Don't argue about this anymore. You don't have to, we'll take care of it."

Actually, the food industry had been trying to get into the American household with processed food for many years before it was accepted. In fact, women rejected processed foods for a long time because they believed it was their responsibility to cook. But once this tension arose, they were offered a solution, and it was an easier solution than forcing men to do their fair share. So both parties were like, Okay, we're gonna let Kellogg's do it—or General Mills, or whomever—and that's going to take the pressure off.

My research suggests that the move away from cooking was in large part a supply-side phenomenon driven by the food industry forcing itself into the home, exploiting this unusual moment in American history when that became possible. You could argue that people are fundamentally lazy, and as soon as someone offers to do a job for them they'll take advantage of it. But reading about that post–World War II era, it's obvious how hard the food industry struggled to get into people's kitchens, and all the rhetorical strategies they needed to do it.

They cleverly adopted the language of feminism. During the seventies, Kentucky Fried Chicken had a billboard all over America. It showed a bucket of fried chicken under the headline WOMEN'S LIBERATION. That was very, very clever marketing. They aligned themselves with this progressive change unfolding in society. So it became a progressive move to buy that bucket of chicken. And men went along with it because it took the pressure off of them. It began after World War II, and it was resisted until the sixties and seventies. McDonald's started in the forties, but wasn't very big until the seventies and eighties. That's when fast food became what a third of American children eat every day.

The supplanting of home cooking by industrial cooking is one of the largest driving forces behind the obesity epidemic and type-2 diabetes in America. Corporations use lots of salt, fat, and sugar because those are cheap ingredients that we like, and which happen to mask the poor quality of processed food. They use lots of novel chemicals to keep processed food from looking nasty, to keep it looking fresher than it is. Chemicals make the food passable and return some of the flavor that's been taken out of the food.

So cooking is a big deal.

Cooking tells the story of humankind. Along with the emergence of language and tools, learning to cook was one of humanity's most important advances. Richard Wrangham, an anthropologist and a primatologist at Harvard, hypothesizes that it was when we learned how to cook—that is, to put meat and other things on a fire—that we really took off as a species. I find his argument compelling. The wellspring of our humanness is the ability to cook. It is what allowed our brains to grow and our guts to shrink. This leap in the size of the human brain allowed us to develop all sorts of cognitive

tools and underlies the development of culture.

Cooking is such a simple technology, but it opened up all these new possibilities. It gave us time that we didn't have before. Animals like apes spend about six hours a day in the act of chewing which really gets in the way of getting things done. One reason primates don't hunt is that they don't have time to do it. All the time our ancestors used to spend chewing, we can now dedicate to music, art, and dance. And when you begin to cook you begin to eat meals as a group. When you're a hunter-gatherer, you basically eat anytime you want or can. But once you begin cooking, you need cooperation—if only to keep the fire going. Cooking leads directly to the shared meal. And sitting down and eating together is an enormous boon to the rise of civilization.

Cooking also gives us access to foods that other animals can't eat—many tubers, for example, are indigestible or poisonous unless cooked. You could argue that other animals cook in a primitive form. They sour things; they ferment seeds. The squirrel that buries the acorn is actually "cooking" it, not just hiding it—it's going through transformations that make it more digestible. Some people believe that dogs bury meat to partially rot it. Rotted food is softer and easier to digest. But cooking over fire unlocks a whole treasure trove of calories that other animals can't get, so it gives humans a huge advantage over other species.

The primal technology of cooking is fire. Cooking over fire

allowed us to make meat more flavorful, as well as to detoxify and sanitize it. The next great leap forward came hundreds of thousands of years later, when we started to cook in clay pots. Pots opened up amazing new possibilities. Once we began cooking in water, we could combine vegetables with one another or with meat; we could soften the least digestible parts of the animal with long, slow cooking. Once we learned to boil water, we could make beer. Around the same time we invented beer, we also started making cheese and bread. These technologies of cooking—along with a handful of others—remained more or less unchanged until the nineteenth century.

Have we invented cooking technologies since then that are anywhere near as beneficial? I think it's doubtful. At a certain point we crossed over from making food more nourishing, more digestible, and more delicious to having the opposite effect.

At what point did we start making food worse instead of better?

Up until the nineteenth century, the history of cooking was all in the direction of making food more nutritious. But in the late nineteenth century, we learned how to refine grain and make white flour. In the 1880s, in England, we came up with roller mills, which can cleanly separate the endosperm—the pure starch—from the germ and bran, which is where most of the nutrients are.

With that "advance," we began taking cooking too far. (Around the same time, we learned how to do something similar with sugar—turning cane and beets into pure sugar.) Cooking essentially went overboard. It began contributing to public health problems. We started to have problems with tooth decay, with obesity, with nutrient deficiencies, because people began to eat lots of empty calories.

We basically got too smart for our own good; we moved from cooking to "food processing." When people talk about processed food as being unhealthy, what they're really talking about is cooking as it is performed by corporations. Companies cook in a different way. They're trying to make food that our bodies can absorb as quickly as possible. You could argue that this process is continuous with the history that I've been describing, which is to make food progressively easier to digest. But at that point they've removed all the fiber, and they're satisfying only the most basic desire for glucose, for sugar.

We love sugar. We're hardwired to like sweetness. It's one of the few food instincts we have. We don't like bitter, because it's usually a sign of a plant toxin. Most of the toxins in nature are bitter; they're alkaloids. We're attracted to sugar because in nature, sugar is a sign of calories, of concentrated energy. In nature, sweetness is a pretty reliable guide to healthy food. It indicates the presence of ripe fruit, which comes with fiber and lots of important nutrients and phytochemicals. But once you've crossed over and you're making processed sugar, it no longer comes with all those good things.

One of the main problems is that there are really two of us

to feed: there's our brain, which loves glucose, and then there's our gut—the microbiome—which has very different dietary needs than "we" do. We really like sugar, but the gut really likes fiber and other parts of plants. We got really good at finding sugar because the brain lives on glucose, but we neglect the fact that you have to feed the whole body, that we're not just eating for one: we're eating for the ten trillion

microbes living inside us. So in our cooking, we have to learn to cook for all ten trillion. But it's hard for us to listen to the desires of those ten trillion—the brain is much easier to hear.

At the turn of the century, white flour became a huge part—something like 20 percent—of the diet. In the early years of the twentieth century, people recognized that white flour was making us sick because of its lack of vitamins. But the beauty of white flour is that it meshes so well with our capitalist economy. It's a commodity that is imperishable. It is largely indistinguishable: all white flour is white flour. White flour can be transported over great distances, it's easier to cook with, it lends itself to industrialized baking; it's a perfect capitalist commodity.

Capitalism is most concerned with food not being perishable, being shelf stable. Whole grains make volatile, perishable flour, so big companies don't want to rely on it. Instead, they figured out a techno fix: supplementation. They said, Okay, these are the vitamins we lost when we took away the bran and the germ, so we'll just put them back in in chemical form. Various B vitamins, niacin, thiamine, all those things. And that took care of the problem. Sort of. It took care of the problem for us, but not for the ten trillion. Your microbes didn't care much about the vitamins; they wanted the bran.

In the history of food processing, you never turn back, you just come up with a technological fix for whatever problems you've created. Food gets more and more complex, more processed. The food industry has established a financial model where you take raw materials—corn, soy, wheat—and you "add value" by creating processed foods from those cheap building blocks. So instead of selling nutritious brown rice, we genetically engineered white rice that has vitamin A in it: "golden" rice. The more complex you can make a food product, the more profitable it is. But at the end of the day, all that processing and engineering is achieving is returning what we took out in the first place. Baby formula is the great example. Breast milk is the perfect food, formed by natural selection to have everything the developing child—and its microbiota—needs. We've spent almost two hundred years trying to simulate it, because food companies can't make money when people are nursing their babies.

But we *still* can't make formula as good as breast milk. There's still that mystery X factor, because babies raised on formula simply don't do as well. When we simulate formula, we try to design what the baby needs and once again we forget about the ten trillion. Only in the last ten years or so did we discover that the oligosaccharides (a kind of sugar) in mother's milk—a "nutrient" that the baby can't digest—are vital to a baby's gut microbes. They encourage the proliferation of bifida, a very important kind of bacteria. It's human arrogance to think we can outwit nature.

How do we go about fixing what we've messed up? Is it all bad news?

I sometimes find myself wondering whether we can posit or imagine a food science that is actually *improving* food in the way that cooking for most of

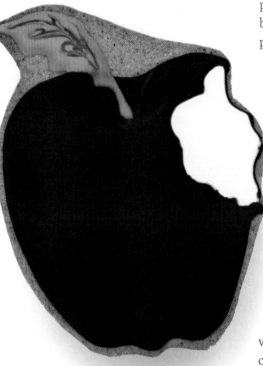

its history succeeded in doing. Theoretically, we should be able to do this. We came up with fermentation; we came up with cooking with fire. We've had food science and food technology now for 150 years, and so far, *not* so good. So far we haven't done anything that useful. But we understand a lot more, and we should be able to improve on

things, not just make money and entertain people.

I can think of some examples of potentially useful food-processing innovations. Here's one that some people are actually working on. For reasons having to do with both our health and the health of our environment, we need really good meat substitutes. So far meat substitutes are really unsatisfying. No one but a vegan can get excited about fake bacon. They seem to think it's really good. But most people who've actually eaten bacon? They don't really see the point. It's probably because vegans have forgotten how real bacon tastes, but they have this deep memory of the experience that is stirred by the fake bacon. Mock-meat hamburgers are not very satisfying, either. They're also much more expensive than real hamburgers, which is odd considering they're made from vegetable matter.

Today there are people using the most sophisticated food science to simulate meat, and it seems to me that if this is done well, it has enormous potential to contribute to our welfare and to the environment. Cheese that is not made with cow's milk might be something to work on because we're consuming huge amounts of the stuff, and dairy cows, like beef cows, have an enormous environmental footprint. The whole California Central Valley—especially Tulare County—is wall-to-wall dairy cows producing low-quality milk for low-quality cheese that's put on Domino's pizzas all over the world.

Synthesizing this type of cheese is really not a very high bar to hit: all that's needed is something white and cheeselike that melts. It seems to me that a good nondairy cheese would be a positive contribution to humankind, and something worth working on.

As a society, this is a very important question we need to pose. How can we cook better—better for our health, and better for the health of the planet? Now we have molecular gastronomy, which is using lots of new techniques. But what has it really contributed? More in the way of novel experiences and entertainment, I would say, and very little toward solving any kind of public health problem. I haven't seen anything in that world that says to me, *If we popularize this technique, it would have really positive effects.* But this is what we need to work on. I have little doubt that if Nathan Myhrvold set that as his goal, he could help solve some of our real nutritional and environmental problems linked to food. But I don't see that happening right now.

Yet there are reasons to feel encouraged. People are much more conscious of food politics and agricultural politics than they were a few years ago. The farm bill used to be just passed without anyone outside of the farm belt noticing. Now we see front-page articles about agricultural policy. We're making some progress toward politicizing things that were once

happening behind closed doors, and that's a good thing.

But we have a long way to go. I want to see the FDA ban antibiotics. I want to see a farm bill that subsidizes healthy food and not just junk food. All that hasn't come yet. The food movement is still a young movement. I'm optimistic, and I don't think we should be discouraged. We're talking about some really entrenched and powerful interests

that need to be dislodged. You look at other comparable movements—the environmental movement or civil rights—and you see that change didn't happen in a decade; it took generations. And this will take generations, too.

The food movement needs strong leadership. There are too many writers and chefs, and not enough smart politicians. We

don't yet have the skills we need to organize and force change in Washington. That said, I do think that chefs are playing a really constructive role. They have the cultural microphone right now, and they're using it to promote good farming and careful thought about food. Part of what we need and what chefs are promoting is the cultural reevaluation of food: recognizing that food is important both to your health and to your culture, and that it's worth spending a little money on it if you can.

What I'm trying to do in my new book [*Cooked*] is make a case for cooking as a valuable way to spend your time. I want to lure people into the kitchen with the promise of pleasure, and not because it's an obligation or something you *should* do. I happen to believe cooking is as interesting as watching TV or being on the computer, which is what people seem to be doing with the time they "save" by not cooking. Cooking isn't drudgery. It takes real mental engagement; it offers sensual pleasures; it's very enriching to cook. My book has all these detours into microbiology and the science of flavor because truly amazing things are going on when you cook. As a cook, you are a chemist and you are a physicist and you are a cultural historian all at once. And what can seem boring to people is often just a failure to use their imaginations and intellect to understand what's actually going on, what is at stake.

It's the same with gardening. Cooking and gardening to me are very similar activities on many levels; you could argue that pulling weeds is boring and you'd rather be looking at a screen. But I usually feel better after I've weeded my garden than after plowing through another hour's worth of e-mail. Ironically enough, I think there is actually more mental space for this kind of work now—our lives are so mediated by technology, so mediated by screens, that there's a real hunger to recover the use of our hands, and our senses.

We're sensorially deprived right now in modern life. Our eyes are engaged—sometimes our ears—but our bodies? Not so much. These aren't just bags of bones we're carrying around. When we cook, when we garden, when we make things with our hands, we're engaging all of our senses and that has—in ways we don't really know how to quantify—deeply positive effects on our mental and physical health. We're hungry for all the complex sensory information that cooking can provide when approached in the right spirit.

What will it take to get people back into the kitchen?

Luring people into the kitchen is something you would hope that the celebration of cooking in the media will do, but I'm worried it's having the opposite effect. Cooking on TV might be keeping people away from

the kitchen. The thing about TV is that it's never about motivating people to do anything but watch more TV. The goal of all TV is to pin you to the couch so you don't turn it off. TV only makes money if they can get you to sit there and watch their advertisements. They want to motivate you to buy things, *maybe* go to the mall. Cooking shows make cooking look difficult, because everything is so fast, and there's always a ticking clock. In real life there isn't a clock when you're cooking unless you're working in a restaurant. The only reason cooking on TV has to happen in fifteen or thirty minutes is to build drama. It has nothing to do with real cooking. And I worry it's keeping people from doing it, which is too bad. Because cooking on television, approached in a different spirit, could be inspiring rather than daunting.

Food porn is a lot like other kinds of porn. It becomes a vicarious experience, not a direct experience. Does porn really motivate people to have sex? The opposite is true, and I think something similar is happening with the spectacle around food. It's not motivating people. It looks too daunting.

Those of us who tell stories in the culture need to celebrate cooking. That's one thing I can do. I'm a storyteller, not a policy maker. There's a lot I can't do. But it seems to me Michelle Obama could have a positive effect here, in the same way she inspired people to garden. Millions of people planted vegetable gardens because of her. She has a little more

trouble talking about home cooking because she doesn't do it, yet she could celebrate the institution of the family meal.

A big part of the problem with cooking in the fifties and sixties was isolation. Cooking alone can be unpleasant and boring. If you look back through history, cooking was very often a cooperative activity. Whether you're talking about managing the fire or several generations of women in the kitchen preparing food, when we moved to this nuclear family, men went off to work, grandparents were banished to Florida, women were cooking by themselves, and kids were no longer forced to help. I think that was a big mistake—pushing everybody out of the kitchen. I enjoy cooking most when I'm doing it with other people. There's nothing better than a dinner party where the guests arrive several hours early

and everybody pitches in before sitting down together. The food never tastes so good as when everybody at the table worked on it and everybody knows what went into it.

We need to bring that sense of communality back into our cooking. I think the best way to get people back into the kitchen is to have more than one person cooking. Husbands and wives, together. Husbands and husbands. Wives and wives. Cooking together. And, of course, kids too. Therein lie the pleasures of cooking.

How would you respond to the argument that cooking is inefficient, or a waste of time?

Most of us produce one thing in our jobs that we sell into the economy, and then we buy everything else. The economy values the virtues—particularly the efficiency—of specialization. Soon after the recession hit, the Zagats wrote an op-ed piece in the *Wall Street Journal* that suggested that, if you want to help the economy, instead of cooking, you should stay later at work doing whatever it is you do well, and then go to a restaurant and let them do what they do well. That's the classic argument for specialization—produce the one thing you do best, and outsource everything else.

I take another view. I think one solution to the big problems we face is people taking responsibility for more aspects of their lives, even if it's economically "inefficient" to do so. One of the reasons we have

so much trouble imagining another way of living that is dramatically less fossil-fuel dependent—the end of the world as we know it—is that we are so fossil-fuel dependent. Wendell Berry calls it "the cheap energy mind," and it's debilitating—we simply can't imagine providing for ourselves. I think achieving a greater degree of self-reliance allows us to begin imagining another way of life,

which is what we now very much need to do.

People who have a vegetable garden are better prepared for the day when gas is six dollars a gallon and food is hard to find. All acts of making—gardening, sewing, knitting, and, of course, cooking—are part of weaning ourselves from a system that is heavily dependent on fossil fuel and that is wrecking the planet. I'm not a survivalist. I'm not preaching going back to complete independence. Interdependence is very important, but it should happen on a different scale: bakers giving extra bread to their neighbors, canners sharing their preserves. Every gardener I know is always trying to get rid of zucchini.

So there's hope for us yet?

I am generally hopeful. People are beginning to rebel against the ways in which we've increased our dependence on corporations to provide for us. The food movement has its problems, and its struggles will probably increase. But it offers people so much. Fighting for environmental causes can be really discouraging. The food movement offers pleasure in the fight. It's one of those rare instances where the right choice is usually the more pleasurable choice, where you can align your ethics and your hedonism. Tell me: where else in life do you get to do that? LP

On Cans

Another transmission from HAROLD MCGEE'S ORBITAL DESK in OUTRÉ SPACE

TONY MILLIONAIRE

As a resident of earthquake country, I've long maintained a sizable stash of emergency canned goods. I buy tuna and beans and chili by the case at big-box stores and store them in trash cans in my backyard. I used to keep track of their best-by dates and replace them regularly. And then a few years ago I heard about vintage canned sardines, and I tasted prized, pricey Galician *conservas*. (Leave it to the French and Spanish to recognize the gastronomic potential of sterilization!) Now I think of best-by dates as maybe-getting-interesting-by dates. And to my trash can of aging staples I've added some hand-packed delicacies, to make sure that survival includes at least a few little pleasures.

It was a French chef and confectioner who started preserving foods with heat and airtight containers, so of course he cared as much about the quality of the result as he did about its longevity. At the beginning of the nineteenth century—decades before anything was known about microbes—Nicolas Appert thought the key to preservation was protecting foods from the air, and based his heating times mainly on what he considered culinarily appropriate for particular foods. He called for partly cooking foods in ordinary pots and pans, then transferring them to glass jars, corking the brim-filled jars, and finishing the cooking in a boiling water bath. Broths and gravies could be cooked for an extra hour without suffering, Appert wrote, "but there are articles which will sustain a great injury from a quarter of an hour's or even a minute's too much boiling. Thus the result will always depend upon the dexterity, intelligence, and judgment of the operator."

English and French inventors, and Appert himself, soon improved on his original method by replacing the fragile glass and corks with more durable metal cans, and the water bath with pressure cookers. Appertization wasn't foolproof—foods sometimes spoiled and cans exploded—but it worked well enough that European navies of the day quickly adopted canned supplies. Some cans lasted more than a century. In 1938, an English chemist reported on his analysis of several from a Royal Navy expedition to the Arctic in 1824; they had been brought back unopened and kept in a museum. The scientists didn't actually sample and describe the beef and tripe and carrots themselves, but they did report that the foods looked and smelled right and that lab rats ate them with gusto and no ill effects.

But it wasn't until after 1895 that canned food became the reliable product it is now. A scion of the Underwood family—canning pioneers in the United States—consulted an MIT chemist named Samuel C. Prescott—later the founding president of the Institute of Food Technologists—about exploding cans of clams. Their experiments revealed the presence of heat-resistant bacteria whose inactivation required raising the can center to a minimum of 250°F and holding it there for at least ten minutes. That finding set the standard modern protocol for canning low-acid foods.

This punishing heat treatment helps create the distinctive flavors of canned goods. So does the hermetically sealed container, which means that after any preliminary cooking outside the can—tuna is steamed to remove moisture, for example, and the best French sardines are lightly fried—oxygen can play only a limited role in flavor development, and that whatever happens in the can stays in the can—no aromas can escape. Hence the common presence of a sulfurous quality, which may be eggy or meaty or oniony or cabbagy or skunky, from compounds like hydrogen sulfide, various methyl sulfides, and methanethiol. Some of these notes can gradually fade during storage as the volatiles slowly react with other components of the food.

The overall flavor is nothing like freshly cooked foods. Food technologists often refer to it as "retort off-flavor." But it's only off in comparison to the results of ordinary cooking. It's really just another kind of cooked flavor, an extremely cooked flavor, and it can be very good. Canned tuna, sardines, chicken spread, and Spam all have their own appeal.

A few intriguing foods are sealed in cans without extreme cooking. The most infamous is Swedish *surströmming*, barrel-fermented herring that continues to ferment in the can, which swells with profoundly offensive gases and becomes hazardous to transport. Easier going and easier to find in North America is Cougar Gold cheese, which has been canned since the 1940s in the creamery at Washington State University in Pullman. It's not like Velveeta or other processed cheese products—cooked slurries of various anonymous cheeses and emulsifying salts. The WSU dairy students make a regular cheddar curd and then seal it in cans, which are kept and sold refrigerated. The various lactic acid bacteria don't need oxygen to survive, and their enzymes slowly develop the cheese's flavor. Fans of Cougar Gold age their cans for years, sometimes decades. But because everything stays in the can, moisture included, the flavor and texture are unlike a true cheddar's. My first bite reminded me of the aroma of canned chicken spread. Incongruous, but it grew on me.

Standard canned goods aren't generally deemed age-worthy. Food technologists define shelf life not by how long it takes for food to become inedible, but how long it takes for a trained sensory panel to detect a "just noticeable difference" between newly manufactured and stored cans. There's no consideration of whether the difference might be pleasant in its own way or even an improvement— it's a defect by definition.

As far as I can tell, European connoisseurship in canned goods goes back about a hundred years. It was well established by 1924, when James H. Collins compiled *The Story of Canned Foods*. Collins noted that while American industry—which started in the 1820s and took off during the Civil War—focused on mechanization and making locally and seasonally abundant seafood and vegetables more widely available, the European industry continued to rely on handwork and produced luxury goods for the well-off, who would age their canned sardines for several years like wine. Today, Rödel and Connetable, both over 150 years old, are among the sardine makers that mark select cans with the fishing year and note that the contents "are already very good, but like grand cru wines, improve

with age" for up to ten years.

But the appreciation of can-aged foods wasn't unknown in the U.S. Collins recounts an informal taste test conducted by a New York grocer who rounded up old cans from a number of warehouses, put on a luncheon in which he served their contents side by side with those from new cans, and asked his guests to choose which version they preferred. Among the test foods were fourteen-year-old pea soup and beef stew, and twelve-year-old corned beef and pigs' feet. The guests preferred the old cans "by an overwhelming majority."

There must be many such minor treasures forgotten in kitchen cabinets and basements and emergency stashes all over the country. My own supply still being fairly young, I consulted the eminent Sacramento grocer Darrell Corti, who very kindly shared a few items from his storeroom. I compared a new can of French sardines in olive oil with 2000 and 1997 *millésimes*. The brands were different, and so were the size and color of the fish and the quality of the olive oils. That said, the young sardines were firm and dry and mild; the older vintages were fragile to the point of falling apart, soft and rich in the mouth, and fishier in a good way. A 2007 can of Spam was also softer than the 2012, less bouncy and less immediately and stingingly salty, though the aromas were pretty much the same. Corti Brothers mincemeat aged for a year under a cap of suet was delicious, its spices and alcohols seamlessly integrated. A five-year-old tin of French goose foie gras: no complaints. Two vintages of Corti Brothers bergamot marmalade: the older noticeably darker in color and surprisingly reminiscent of Moroccan preserved lemons. And three-year-old Cougar Gold—still moist and not as sharp as open-aged cheddars—was deeper in color and flavor than the yearling version, with a touch of caramel and the crunchy crystals that are the hallmark of hard aged Goudas.

The trouble with aging canned goods is that it takes years to get results. However, we can take a hint from manufacturers, who often accelerate shelf-life tests by storing foods at high temperatures. A general rule of thumb is that the rate of chemical reactions approximately doubles with each 20°F rise in temperature. Store foods at 40° above normal—around 100°F—and you can get an idea of a year's change in just three months.

But it's possible to go further. At 120°F, you get a year's worth of change in six weeks; at 140°F, three weeks; at 180°F, five days.

Of course temperatures that high are cooking temperatures, and their heat energy drives reactions that would never occur in normal storage. But if we're interested in the evolution of canned foods, which have already been extremely cooked, then why not treat them to a little additional simmering and see what happens? (It's safest to stay a little below the boil, to avoid building up steam pressure in the can.)

I've found that braising cans changes the flavors and textures within, but unpredictably so. It doesn't seem to do much for sardines, but tuna in water loses its beefiness and becomes more pleasantly fishy and also a little bitter, while tuna in oil somehow gets more meaty and less fishy. Like its aged version, can-braised Spam takes on a softness that's especially nice when you fry the surface to a crunchy crust.

I don't recommend cooking foods in the can as a routine thing. Cans have various linings that may gradually release unwanted chemicals into foods, and this process will also accelerate at high temperatures. But it's a way to explore how canned foods are capable of developing.

I do hope that some restless, frontier-seeking food lovers will look past our present happy surfeit of small-batch pickles and fruit preserves and try their hands at canning age-worthy meats and fish. This could be done Appert-style in mason jars, but it's also a chance to combine cooking with metalwork, as some French cooks have done. Jules Gouffé's 1869 *Book of Preserves* simply directs the cook to solder lids on tins for a number of fish, meat, and vegetable preparations, and the 1938 edition of the *Larousse Gastronomique* does the same for foie gras.

And there are some things you could really only put up in metal. According to the early canning chroniclers A.W. and K.G. Bitting, in 1852, Raymond Chevallier-Appert presented to the French Society for the Encouragement of National Industry an entire sheep, already a year in the can.

Vintage head-to-tail: now there's inspiration for rethinking the can, and the stash-worthy. Ⓛ

CANADIAN SPAM

With macaroni and olives | *Makes 1 can (about 6 servings)*

Brine the ham → Process the meats → Mix together → Can and cook → Fry SPAM; serve

"I grew up with a fishing family on the ocean in Campbell River, British Columbia, watching my dad smoke and can salmon and oysters, while my mom was inside pickling cucumbers and carrots," Derek Dammann tells me.

At his restaurant, Maison Publique, in Montreal, Dammann cooked up a less pastoral image: faux SPAM. Unlike the real deal, it's not shelf stable, nor does it improve with age. Like Martin Picard's legendary *Canard en Conserve*— aka Duck in a Can—the can is for aesthetic purposes only.

"The end result should be cooled, kept refrigerated, and used as close to processing time as possible," Dam-

mann explains. "Pressure canning these ingredients would involve another process and method, yielding a very different result."

This version of SPAM also co-opts another classic from the forcemeat canon. Once cooked and sliced, Derek's SPAM resembles "the coolest loaf of all—you know, the Oscar Mayer one with pimentos in it." Granted, you may have had to grow up in Canada to appreciate the reference, but that's the case with most Canadian humor, isn't it?

—ALEXANDRA FORBES

INGREDIENTS & EQUIPMENT

7 oz	fresh ham, cut into large cubes
5 drops	red food coloring
3 drops	yellow food coloring
3½ oz	fatty pork belly, cut into large cubes
½ C	ice, plus extra to keep things cold
3½ oz	lean pork, cut into large cubes
¾ t	salt
¼ t	Instacure #1 (pink curing salt)
2 t	smoked paprika
½ t	freshly ground black pepper
½ C	Manzanilla olives stuffed with pimentos, rinsed
½ C	macaroni, cooked on the "under" side of al dente
+	canner and a #1 can, or wide-mouth jars (the jar opening should be flush with the walls of the jar)
+	immersion circulator, or at least a thermometer to monitor water temperature

HAM BRINE

4¼ C	water
¾ C	salt
1	clove
1 clove	garlic, crushed
1	bay leaf
4	juniper berries

1 **Heat all brine ingredients** in a nonreactive pot until salt is dissolved. Chill thoroughly.

2 **Submerge the cubed ham** in the brine for a minimum of 12 hours and a max of 24 hours. Rinse off and pat dry before using.

3 **Weigh out the other ingredients** and place them in separate containers (the meats in metal bowls over a bin full of ice so they stay cold).

4 **In a food processor,** pulse the ham and the food coloring until it's ground fine and has that signature SPAM color. Scrape out the purée, and keep it cold.

Purée the belly next; set it aside. Pulse the ice to break it up a bit; set it aside, too.

6 **Process the lean pork** with the salts until it becomes pasty. The salt will pull out the proteins in the meat, which aids emulsification. Add half the ground ice and process until smooth. Toss in the belly paste and process for another minute. Add the rest of the ice and process until

smooth and shiny, like mayonnaise.

7 **Transfer the porky paste** to a large bowl. Add the puréed ham, paprika, and black pepper. Stir with a spatula until the texture is uniform and the spices are evenly dispersed. Fold in the macaroni and olives.

8 **Fill your can or jar** with the pork mixture. Give it a few strong taps on the counter to make sure it's packed as tightly as possible. Seal it. Maison Publique uses a home can sealer—not a commercial one.

Cook the can in a water bath with an immersion circulator set at 155°F for 3 hours. If you don't have a circulator, keep the water at or just above 155°F. Once cooked, submerge the can or jar in an ice bath until it's cool, then refrigerate overnight.

9 **Open the can and extract the SPAM.** Cut into thick slices. Eat as is, or sauté until crisp on both sides. Serve with lightly dressed Brussels sprout leaves, atop a slice of aged cheddar and a piece of toasted brioche. Keep it in the fridge, and eat it within a few days.

*Purée the pork into a smooth, uniform paste before folding in the pasta (**step 7**).*

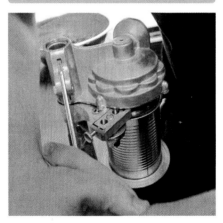

*No canner? Torque the meat into a plastic-wrapped torchon (**step 8**).*

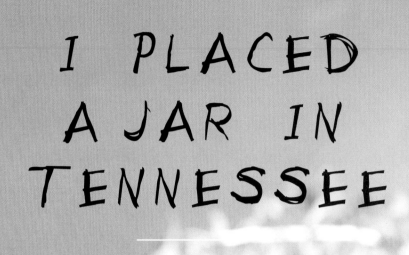

I PLACED A JAR IN TENNESSEE

A peculiar case of reinvention
through preservation

JOHN JEREMIAH SULLIVAN

In the yard of the house I grew up in—I'm looking at it right now on Google Maps, satellite and street views open in simultaneous windows (plus a real estate site that's telling me it wasn't even a full half acre of land)—there grew three fruits. The man who'd built the house was a priest. Our priest, actually, at St. Paul's Episcopal downtown. He baptized me. His name was Fallis, pronounced like "phallus." The doctor who delivered and circumcised me was called Hymen. The Fallis family would have been the ones to plant the trees and bushes, sometime in the fifties. Whether meaning to or not, they'd bequeathed some culture to our small sector of the rolling tract-house development. In the backyard we had a mature peach tree that my mother would visit on summer mornings. She'd slice off pieces onto our cereal. There was also an apple tree, with some variety of bitter cooking apple that nobody in our family knew how to prepare—tiny ones, bright green with a brushstroke of barn red when they were ripe. The fruit all went to waste. But at least we watched it grow and talked now and then about how a person might use the apples, my mother confident that there were "people who could tell you how to do it."

About the third fruit, the quinces that grew on a large bush next to the driveway, nobody ever said anything assuring like that. The quinces were weird. We didn't know what to make of them, figuratively or literally. Did people eat them? They could have come from space. In fact on *Sesame Street* there used to be a skit that involved two aliens. They couldn't reach the fruit on their planet's fruit trees. One alien was too short, the other couldn't bend its arms. When that came on I would glance outside at our quince bush. Extraterrestrial nectarines: that's what they looked like. Beautiful, I realize now. Like a cross between a lemon and pear. (They symbolize fertility.) In the street-view picture, the quince bush was still there, but in the satellite view, taken five years later, you can see it's been mowed to the ground. In the grass where it was there's a pale, almost perfect circle.

I hadn't thought of the quince bush for a couple of decades until I visited an old friend in LA last year, one I'd kept in contact with but hadn't seen in several years. I'd flown into town that afternoon and was supposed to leave at dawn—it was one of those situations where it made no sense to go to sleep. You'd just be torturing yourself. Kevin West: a friend from college. We were in his apartment in Koreatown, a nice pad with a view of the city lights, though noticeably smaller than his old place in Laurel Canyon. He'd recently downsized his life. He had a bottle of good rye whiskey and some olives. At one point he was explaining to me that all modern fruit preserving, in cans and jars, descends from a discovery the Romans made—that if you cooked the otherwise inedible quince in honey and sealed it in jars, it became sweet and made excellent jam. Quince in honey, as a preserve, spread all over the world. The Portuguese called it *marmelada*. Marmalade.

Kevin showed up at our small school in Tennessee as a junior, seeming somehow older. He'd spent the preceding couple of years at Deep Springs, the college out West where you grow your own food and herd cattle on horseback while debating Aristotle. Before that he'd grown up in an actual holler, in East Tennessee, where his family had been settled for nearly 150 years. His self-described "flower child" mother nurtured his love of books and shells. But he had a fashion thing going, too. In my first memory-image of him, he's walking across the quad in safari shorts and a purple neckerchief, his hair as it remains, full-bodied butterscotch. Carrying some kind of satchel. He drove a tiny yellow diesel car and could roll a cigarette with one hand, pouch to flame. Within days one of the wittier campus wags had dubbed him the Jolly Rancher.

But meeting him, the word pretentious never entered *my* head. He was too clearly doing Kevin, both doing and inventing him. Two paths were open when he graduated—studying classical languages at Berkeley, or becoming an assistant at *Vogue*. He chose the latter and moved to New York, soon getting hired at *W* magazine, where he became their Paris editor. For years you'd talk to him on the phone and he'd just have come back from staying on an island with models somewhere. He partied on separate instances with Prince Charles and Puffy (in the latter case somehow smuggling in a bunch of fellow Deep Springs alums dressed like hippie hobos—the woman at the rope looked dubious until Tom Ford appeared in a velvet jacket and swept them all inside). Hearing his stories, I always pictured old Alfa Romeo Spiders like the one in *Contempt*. "Swimming swimming, sun golden," was Kevin's characteristically gerundive description of these lost weekends.

I won't lie, it was strange to imagine him out there among the pretty people. Not that he didn't belong, couldn't pull it off, but when I knew him best, he was a bookish person. That's how we connected. A mutual friend of ours talked about finding him in the quad one day in tears because a professor was inside "destroying" one of his favorite books. He'd been compelled to run out of the room. When we talked, it was mostly about Shakespeare's sonnet sequence, which he was obsessed with in those days. He had a hopeless confused crush on a beautiful lesbian woman. How was that Kevin surviving the inevitable moral obscenities of the ultra rich? It was impossible not to suspect that the old scholar/seeker/cowboy person was getting... not bored, but restless.

He got depressed. He dropped out of the "mag world." He was more or less stranded in California, where he'd been working as *W*'s West Coast editor for a while but had no roots. He started feeling a gut-level homesickness that made him physically ill. But like most of us, he didn't really want to go home. "Do you know that song," he asked, "'How Ya Gonna Keep 'Em Down on the Farm (After They've Seen Paree)'?"

It wasn't east Tennessee he missed, anyway. Not the physical place, in other words. It was something about the life he'd known there, the feeling of your everyday reality being in sync with the natural world in a way that went beyond daytime/nighttime. He found himself thinking a lot about his grandparents' farm. His grandmother had been "a pretty active preserver," he

SEVILLE ORANGE MARMALADE

Makes 6 ½ pints

INGREDIENTS

| 5 lbs Seville oranges | 3½ qts water | 5 lbs organic sugar |

Seville orange marmalade tastes like nothing else. The flavor is intense, oily, penetrating, and almost spicy. You'll sense oranges in your sinuses for minutes afterward. I'm crazy for it, but I don't give it to friends without first checking that they like real marmalade. A fellow marmalade fanatic puts it this way: I like to taste the peel.

The raw Seville—or sour—orange is nearly inedible. Until cheap sugar became widely available in relatively recent times, *Citrus aurantium* was valued principally for its intensely fragrant peel and blossoms, which are the source of orange flower water. Some cultures use the tart juice in cooking as a souring agent, the way one might use lemon juice. Boiling the peels, though, makes them supple and extracts pectin and water-soluble bitter phenols. With the addition of ample sugar, the bitter-sweet balance comes into a tense equilibrium, and the result is explosively exciting. Given the sour orange's high acidity (which kills pathogenic bacteria, including those that cause botulism) and the preservative effect of sugar (which locks up "free" water, rendering it useless for water-seeking microbes), marmalade is the most durable of all sweet preserves. Think of it this way: what prosciutto is to a raw pork leg, marmalade is to raw Seville oranges— a leap toward immortality, both a delicacy and a preserve.

This is a big-batch recipe. As given, it will require a large 10-quart preserving pan. You should halve the quantities to fit smaller pans. For the sake of time management, I suggest how to divide the work over two days, although an overnight soak isn't strictly necessary so long as you thoroughly cook the whole fruit.

During the brief, mid-winter harvest, Seville oranges can sometimes be found at ethnic markets. *Ripetoyou.com* ships them fresh from California groves.

—KEVIN WEST

said, meaning of fruits and meat but more than that, too. "She wouldn't have thought of herself this way," he said. "Part of farm life was 'putting up' food." She had a pantry full of hams and bacon. "That part of Tennessee didn't get electricity till the forties," he said, "so within living memory you had a food culture that went back to the pre-industrial age." He had nice memories of his grandmother's pickled beets. "Fourteen-day pickles—a fermented pickle. Also, she made this strawberry freezer jam that was really delicious." The canning and jarring moved with the seasons, and within the seasons—you had to pick the fruits and berries at the right time. Every batch was a new little chemistry experiment. Things could go wrong. You were always monitoring some jar in the kitchen, observing its changes. It gave the whole house a clock to go by.

One day Kevin was getting ready to have people over for dinner—this was about four years ago—and wanted to serve strawberries for dessert. He drove to the Santa Monica farmers' market and bought a giant flat of ripe strawberries, ten pounds, many times beyond what his guests would eat. At home he looked down at these beautiful berries, realizing with that sort of animistic empathy a child can feel for nonanimal objects that half of them would probably go to rot, and he thought for the first time in many years about the strawberry jam. Waking up the next day, hungover, he started

trying to make it. Called home for help with the recipe. Cooked the fruit in sugar.

"Fruit cooked with sugar equals preserves," he said. "The jam was a total mess. Edible, just not very good."

If he could make it taste as good as hers had, recreate the flavor and texture, that would be to carry forward that old life, bringing it into his world. A thread of connection. So he felt.

These days when you say someone becomes "obsessed" with something it usually means they spent four hours reading about it on the Internet last night, but it seems accurate to say that Kevin became obsessed with preserves. It gradually became not the only thing he talked about, but the thing you could tell he was always thinking about. He started making cross-country trips to track down fruits that supposedly "put up" well. He tried to preserve things he'd never seen preserved, stuff that would have made his grandmother have to lie down and fan herself. He sent me a picture of a Buddha's hand citron one time. It was an unearthly yellow and looked like a squid. If one of the ghosts in Pac-Man had been bright yellow and was preserved in a specimen jar, where it got all distended over time, it would have looked like this thing. "Found this last night at the Altadena farmer's market," he wrote. "My first thought was, I wanna get that, I wanna preserve it."

1 Scrub the oranges in cold water. If using store-bought fruit, also clean them with very hot water to remove all traces of wax.

2 Put the whole fruit in a large kettle and add the water to cover. Bring to a boil, cover tightly and lower the heat to maintain a low simmer for about 90 minutes. Diana Kennedy says that the oranges are done "when the handle of a wooden spoon can easily pierce the rind," and I agree. Remove the oranges with a slotted spoon and lay them out on a baking

sheet to cool for half an hour. Measure the cooking liquid and, if necessary, reduce or add water to make 8 cups. Pour it into a large bowl and set aside.

3 Slice the oranges in half and scoop out the pulp with a spoon. Without being too particular about it, separate the numerous seeds from the mushy pulp and put them in a muslin jelly bag or cheesecloth pouch. Tie off the bag and let it soak in the cooking liquid. Discard the leftover pulp.

He visited libraries to read old recipe books. He took a cooking-chemistry class, at one point, to know more about what was happening to the fruits and vegetables at the molecular level. He connected with other fixated types out in the world of new-primitive preserving. Mainly, though, he was spending hundreds of hours alone in the kitchen experimenting. I would get e-mails from him about his struggles. Jellies were "temperamental," he wrote. They were like young sopranos singing arias: you had to sit there hoping they wouldn't crack. Especially if you didn't use the commercial pectin, which he avoided, preferring to rely on the fruits themselves for their natural supply. But working that way it was "easy to end up with syrup— that's a failure." He made jams, jellies, and other concoctions out of beach plums, cardoons, cushaw, damsons, eggs, elderberries, fennel, horseradish, huckleberries, limettas, medlars, mulberries, and nasturtium pods. He preserved quince: under the guidance of Oregon pickle-jam guru Linda Ziedrich, he made a syrup of quince, not a disaster-accident syrup but a deliberate one, flavored with rose geranium.

It seemed on one level like the kind of life phase your friends go through where you say things like, "Is it making them happy? 'Cause that's all I care about." But over time it grew clear that something deeper was going on. My wife had a student once, in North Carolina, who went off one spring break to intern on a movie set, and in the midst of it the whole department got a very short e-mail from him that read, "Found my passion y'all." That's what had happened.

With this passion there developed another, quasi-ideological, near-survivalist side to Kevin's interest in that old prerefrigerated world. I have one e-mail from him in which he describes the home-preserving culture he'd grown up with as "a template for how to survive in the post-oil/post-global/post-Apocalypse future…"

…grow your own food, preserve it at home, survive. One of the big issues with climate change is where can we secure access to arable land and clean water in order to grow food, and how to develop the personal skills and connect with a local agricultural context that would allow for true food independence— in other words, reinventing village life. It's the Jeffersonian ideal refracted through the dark prism of contemporary pessimism about the future. I think the remnant agrarian communities in the southern Appalachians provide a viable model. By contrast, not far from my dad's place is a demonstration of one of the gravest errors we've made as a nation, which is to take rich farmland out of production by turning it into sterile suburbs. I could show you where my grandparents' farm was sold and turned into a housing development—some of the streets are named after them, which they would have despised. There's actually a spot where John Riley West Road intersects with Eloise West Road. Bitter…

4 **Cut the halved peels in two and then slice each quarter along the bias into strips about ¼" wide by 1½" long.** Add the sliced peel to the bowl of cooking liquid as you work. When all the peels are sliced, you can cover the bowl and put it aside overnight.

5 **Put the peels and liquid in a preserving pan and squeeze the seed bag to extract as much liquid as possible.** Continue to knead the bag for several minutes, "milking" it to extract several tablespoons of a thick, cloudy pectin gel. Add the pectin to the preserving pan. Bring the pan to a full rolling boil and add the sugar, which has been warmed on a cookie sheet in a 250°F oven for 15 minutes. Reduce the mixture over high heat, skimming as necessary and stirring regularly.

6 **After about 45 to 50 minutes, the marmalade will turn glossy and noticeably darker.** Check for a gel set using the cold-saucer method: place a teaspoon of preserve on a chilled saucer in the freezer for one minute. If the puddle of cooled preserve has formed a "skin" that wrinkles when you push your finger through it, you have a gel set. If not, reduce for another two minutes and test again. Allow the marmalade to cool for 5 minutes, stirring a few times, then ladle it into prepared half-pint jars, leaving ¼" headspace. Make sure all the strips of rind are submerged. Run a skewer or other thin implement around the inside edge of the jar to remove any air pockets. Seal and process the jars in a boiling water bath for 10 minutes. Seville orange marmalade will keep for 2 years or more, darkening as it ages. Food historian C. Anne Wilson's *The Book of Marmalade* cites the curious case of a sealed tin of marmalade that was opened nearly 80 years after its manufacture and found to be fresh and delicious.

Kevin has written a book about all of it, called *Saving the Season: A Cook's Guide to Home Canning, Pickling, and Preserving*, to be published this summer by Knopf. Part cookbook, part manifesto, and part crypto-memoir, it's literate and lyrical and fanatically well researched. Also probably quite useful, if you're into home preserving or want to be. Even if you're not, though, it's the kind of cookbook you can read for pleasure. Me, for instance—I can't see doing any canning or jarring anytime soon. I want to, I feel the appeal, but a person should know his limitations, and when you grew up on Pillsbury toaster strudel, for breakfast and sometimes lunch (what the hell), even the simple stages of cooking with sugar, sealing the lid, et cetera, can present real obstacles. Even I was able to enjoy the book. It has more than 200 recipes but is shot through with little essays, too—about preserving, food gathering, gardening, family, and what it means to find a second act.

I ordered a couple of boxes of Kevin's jams and pickles, which he sells and barters in low quantities. Just having them has exerted an effect on the vibe of

ABOVE: a polaroid of young Kevin West by Scott Sternberg; all other photos by Kevin West

our kitchen and by extension the rest of the house. They're like little jars of distilled sunlight, sitting there on the table. Through them I discovered the beauty of really good jam, namely that if you put it on toast— most difficult to ruin of all human foods—suddenly, almost without meaning to, you've started your day off well, with a little moment of flavor worth lingering over. My mother visited and ate some of Kevin's Scotch marmalade, saying it gave her strong Kentucky-childhood flashbacks.

My favorite of all the jars, the one I was saddest to see go down to just those sticky smudges of unscrapeable purple scum on the glass, was the boysenberry jelly. I sent Kevin a message asking him about the history of this fruit, which I'd always thought was made up by energy-drink purveyors to describe vaguely pan-berry flavorings. Kevin replied that its origins were more complicated than that. It had indeed been developed recently, in evolutionary terms, but in the 1920s, by a man named Boysen. He served in the army in World War I, and when it ended, moved with his wife to a small farm in California. There he started experimenting with berry hybrids, mixing pollens. He finally achieved the boysenberry—which tastes, to me, like a quintessence of berryness, with a grape-juicy sweetness, but wide enough on your palate not to seem oversweet. "It's one of the bramble berries," Kevin wrote. "It has an obvious kinship with the wild blackberries I picked growing up."

Boysen tried to make a go of his berry. He even started filling out a patent application. He suffered a freak accident, however—fell fifteen feet and broke his back. The farm on which he'd developed the berry got sold. His berry beds all but disappeared under weeds. Only years later did he receive a visit from two men, one of whom was Walter Knott, of Knott's Berry Farm. They'd heard about Boysen's berry from other farmers who'd tasted it, and wanted to try it themselves. He led them out to the old field, where they were able to salvage a few vines for transplant.

Now Boysen's berries were on my table, in some form, or used to be. While the jar lasted, it seemed expressive of something—that what's old doesn't need to be old-fashioned. It gets reborn. And with patience and skill you can capture it. You can arrest it. **LP**

QUINCE IN HONEY

Makes about 4 pints

I first went quince crazy because of Nostradamus—yes, the same guy whose prophesies read like medieval sci-fi. He was also a confectioner, and his recipes for ruby-red quince jelly sent me out trolling through Armenian markets in LA to find the fabled fruit. Later my shrink gave me a copy of Misette Godard's 1977 cookbook, *Le Temps des Confitures*, which added the modernish accent of black pepper to mix. Her recipe has guided me since. —**KEVIN WEST**

INGREDIENTS

5 lbs	quince
3 lbs (4 C)	honey
3 C	water
*	freshly cracked black pepper

1 Peel the quinces and cut them into eighths. Trim out the woody core and the hard "stone cells" surrounding it, then slice the pieces lengthwise as thinly as possible. Weigh the prepared fruit. You should have about 3 pounds. (Reserve the peels and cores for making jelly.)

2 Combine the honey and water in a saucepan and bring to a boil over high heat. Add the sliced quince and lower the flame to maintain a steady simmer. Periodically turn the fruit over in the syrup, being careful not to break the slices. Skim any foam. After about 30 minutes the quince will begin turning pink. Add six or eight grinds of black pepper.

3 Continue simmering for another 20 minutes or more, until the quince slices are uniformly dark pink and translucent. Loosely pack into prepared jars (washed and warmed in a 250°F oven for 15 minutes), leaving ½" headspace. Run a skewer or other thin implement around the inside edge to remove any air pockets. Seal and process the jars in a boiling water bath for 10 minutes.

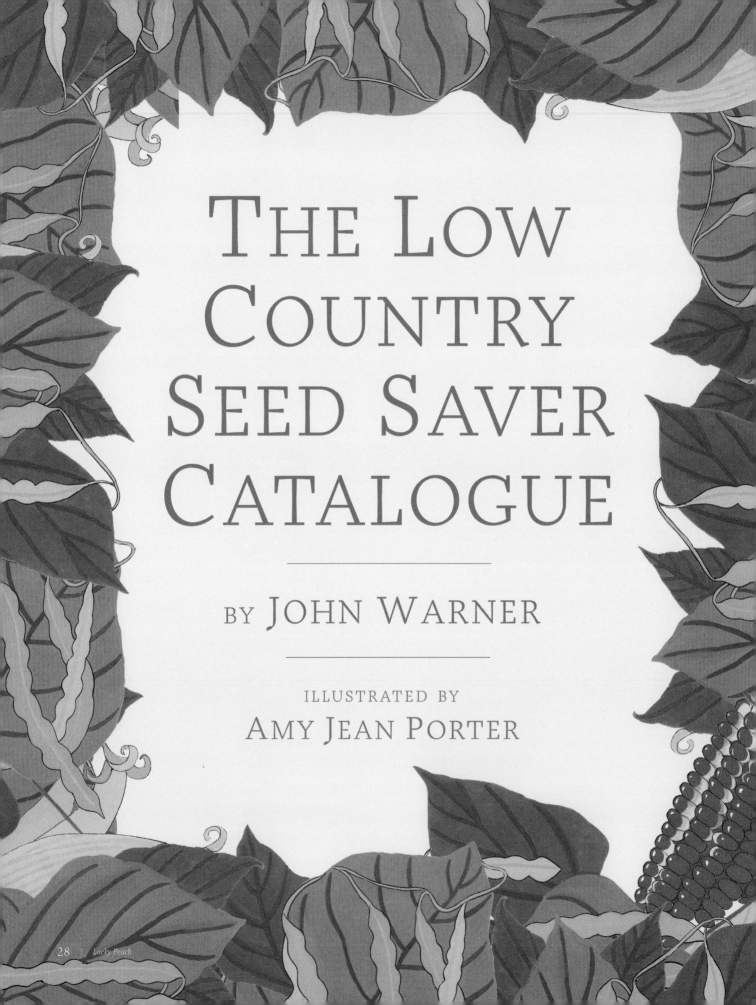

The Low Country Seed Saver Catalogue

by John Warner

ILLUSTRATED BY
Amy Jean Porter

Sean Brock's passion projects live in a lab above McCrady's, one of the two restaurants he oversees in Charleston, SC.

Stainless steel tables ring the perimeter of the 12' x 12' room. In one corner there's half a dozen vats of experimental vinegars. Another table holds a half-constructed still that Brock is excited to get going. A blackboard dotted with ratios and formulas testifies to the latest trials.

In one corner, a chest freezer big enough for a body or two holds the most urgent part of Brock's work. He raises the lid, revealing three inches of caked ice around the rim. It takes almost twenty minutes for him to pull out a fraction of his collection of heirloom seeds.

Seed saving used to be a way of life on America's family farms. Today, many varieties have been lost to large-scale farming focused on yield and seed "consistency" that relies on cloning, rather than open pollination for reproduction.

Five years ago, Brock became inspired by men like Glenn Roberts of nearby Anson Mills, and John Coykendall of Blackberry Farm in Tennessee, who recognized the extinction threat to any number of regional varieties. He joined them in finding, cataloguing, and storing the seeds of once popular vegetables that have disappeared from home and restaurant kitchens throughout the South.

"Now I'm a fucking hoarder," he says, laughing.

(Brock isn't the only one. The Norwegian government has spent millions on the Svalbard Global Seed Vault, located on a remote archipelago 800 miles from the North Pole, where more than 750,000 different seed samples are now stored for posterity.)

The varietals Brock's pulled from his freezer—Jimmy Red Corn, Wild Goose Beans, African Guinea Flint Corn, Sea Island Rice Pea, Bertie Best Greasy Bean—once faced extinction. But by working alongside others like Roberts and Coykendall, Brock is hoping not just to keep these varieties in existence, but to return them to the pantry—and to the table. He has a particular interest in the food of the South Carolina low country—the Sea Islands near Charleston.

"We're letting all these things die which actually have flavor, character, and stories. I believe that when people stop growing food, they stop telling stories. Each seed has a story, the story of its origin—its agricultural history and its uses in the field—but also at the table—its flavor and the way it tastes different from most things that are available today. Sometimes they tell the story of the family."

Brock has stories for all of his seeds—not just the histories attached to the vegetables, but new stories of how he came to acquire them and how he's employed them. What follows is just a sample of his collection.

JIMMY RED CORN

One day, after hearing John Coykendall lament that he'd never again taste the corn he'd grown up with, Brock declared that he wanted to start growing distressed varieties on his restaurants' farmland. To join the ranks of the seedsmen, Brock first had to pass a test.

Glenn Roberts told him about a man named Ted Chewning who had some seed corn he was willing to part with, but only if Brock would hang out with him first, and prove himself worthy of the stock. Brock spent the day with Chewning's family, absorbing and marveling at how they lived off the land, and returned home with a few ears of Jimmy Red. "It was one of those things where you put something in the dirt that has more meaning than food."

Brock took the first harvest, hand shucked and plucked the ears, and ground some seed for a cornbread that he says may be "too intense" for some people because we're so used to tasteless corn. So inspired by the experience, he got an ear of it tattooed on his left forearm: Jimmy Red corn was Brock's first conquest, his entrée into the world of major-league seed savers.

WILD GOOSE BEAN

Seed saving wasn't a completely alien practice to Brock: throughout his childhood in rural Wise County, Virginia, he says it was a way of life. "You did it because it was cheaper and it made sense. If we weren't cooking, we were preserving. If we weren't cooking and preserving, we were in the field. Now I realize how lucky I was to see food in that context."

One of the varieties Brock grew up with was his grandmother Audrey Morgan's Wild Goose beans, the "crown jewel" of her seeds. Three or four months after his grandmother passed, Brock and his mother visited Blackberry Farm. Brock often shares his seeds, and he had given the Wild Goose Bean to Coykendall years earlier, but forgotten that he had. "We were in the garden," Brock says, "and I didn't even know they were growing them, and I looked over and my mom was crying her eyes out and there was a sign right there that said AUDREY MORGAN. To me, that's one of the greatest things about seed saving. It tells the story about a person and who they were."

CAROLINA GOURDSEED WHITE CORN

Glenn Roberts is the son of a "geechie" cook (someone who uses rice as the centerpiece of every meal) from Edisto, SC. He was raised in California, and grew up a polymath: a former music major, air force pilot, and long-haul trucker. He also worked in food, with an interest in history and food preservation. One night in the mid-1990s, after being delivered a sackful of weeviled rice hours before he was supposed to cook an authentic lowcountry dinner, Roberts made it his life's mission to resurrect Carolina Gold Rice.

But before he could start growing rice, he grew corn, because it was easier and cheaper. Not just any corn, though. Roberts went driving through the state, peering into backyards for tall corn. As Brock tells it, "The thing to remember is that Glenn Roberts looks like a federal agent, and these people weren't growing corn because they were making grits." Roberts was browsing moonshiners' crops for signs of Carolina Gourdseed white corn.

Roberts talked one of these old moonshiners out of enough seed to plant thirty acres of corn, taking in his first harvest in 1998. The grits that resulted from the crop "blew minds," and Roberts started Anson Mills, now a thriving commercial provider of heirloom grains to cooks across the country.

CAROLINA GOLD RICE

In 1998, a wide-eyed Sean Brock's first taste of the legendary low-country dish hoppin' John made with "Uncle Ben's and three-year-old cowpeas from a can" made him question what all the fuss was about. Before moving to South Carolina, Brock had fantasized about his first taste of honest-to-goodness hoppin' John. What he found was a pale facsimile of what he'd come to expect. What was missing was Carolina Gold rice. Carolina Gold was once one third of the triumvirate of cotton, indigo, and rice that made Charleston the richest city in the Union prior to the Civil War. African in origin, the long-grain rice grows especially well in the hot South Carolina climate. But by the early nineties, the variety was all but extinct. Now, thanks to the efforts of Glenn Roberts at Anson Mills and the Carolina Gold Foundation, what was once almost gone is now sold in the Charleston airport gift shop.

SEA ISLAND RED PEA

The other half of a plate of hoppin' John is the Sea Island red pea, another variety that Brock planted on his own farm after he found it wasn't available elsewhere. Brock cites the Sea Island red pea's original decline as an example of industry choosing convenience over quality. "We traded deliciousness and nutrition for efficiency. Laziness is going to kill us."

SEA ISLAND RICE PEA

Brock has been dreaming about serving an all-white hoppin' john with Carolina Gold rice and the Sea Island rice pea. Unfortunately, he's experienced firsthand why the Sea Island fell out of favor with commercial growers. Or, as he puts it, he's "fucked it up three years in a row."

"It's just too hot right now, and if you're not on it every minute of the day, it will just burn to a crisp. Friday, it's really, really close; you go away for the weekend and come back and the whole thing is gone—everything is dried up and ruined. It's insane. This year it looked like a Tim Burton movie, this withered-up plant."

WHIPPOORWILL FIELD PEA

"We grew a truckload of this stuff and sat in the kitchen and hulled it by hand. The work that goes into it, taking the plants out of the field and getting them into a jar in a freezer is insane. We're able to do it because we're not farmers, and when we grow stuff it's not to pay the bills," says Brock. He relies on Anson Mills to supply his restaurants so he can give his seeds away, rather than cook them.

Because the Whippoorwill is a small pea, it's lost the popularity contest to its larger cousin, the black-eyed pea. But its fans say that it has a deeper and richer flavor, and it grows tremendously well in the hot southern climate.

BENNE

Benne is another one of the key ingredients that had gone

missing from low-country cuisine. Also grown during the rice era, it was lost to war and "progress." For years, local chefs had been substituting "commodity sesame" for benne, which to Brock is like someone "asking for a banana and being given an apple." Now that it's returned to the kitchen, Brock uses it in dishes like a traditional oyster-benne stew. He'll also blend the benne seeds and Carolina Gold rice into a paste, dehydrate it, fry it, and sprinkle it over the top of the stew.

ANTICA FARRO/ VERDE FARRO

Another difficult crop to harvest, farro is a wheat grain that has to be pulled by hand. When asked how he accomplishes it, Brock laughs and tells me that kitchen or waitstaff who "misbehave" might find themselves on farro duty. The pronounced differences between the Antica and Verde varieties testify to the importance of their preservation. Antica is "subtle" and "light" while Verde is "in your face, nutty, earthy, very robust."

GREASY CUT-SHORT BEAN

Brock often receives seeds from others. One source is the Bradshaw Collection, named for Dr. David Bradshaw, a retired horticulturist at Clemson University. Brock remembers the Greasy Cut-Short from his childhood, when his family would make "leather britches"—strings of beans that decorate Christmas trees. As for the bean itself, Brock says, "What's neat about it is that through the drying process they take on an umami taste, so it's like eating a pot roast."

JOHN HAULK CORN

Another variety from the Bradshaw collection, John Haulk corn remains popular in the rural areas of the South Carolina low country, such as Wadmalaw Island, but also grows well in the foothill region upstate. It's a "dent" corn, making it higher in starch and lower in sugar, with stalks that sometimes grow to fifteen feet. It's also good for animal feed, but Brock likes it for the table. He describes it as "really, really floral," with a "delicate and refined" flavor.

HONEY DRIP SORGHUM

To Brock, growing sorghum is "about community and tradition."

"If you grow sorghum and you live in rural areas, each year you have a sorghum potluck, where everybody gets together and you bring your sorghum, and you press it all together and boil it all down together. It's an all-day affair, sometimes two or three days, and everyone brings a covered dish and everyone hangs out and catches up, and it shows you the cultural part of agriculture. If people stop growing sorghum, these potlucks stop, and that sense of gathering community and friendship goes away."

The flavor of the syrup depends on the degree of malt and how much it's cooked down. Brock likes it rich and dark, but not all the way to molasses.

BERTIE BEST GREASY BEAN

One group dedicated to seed saving is the Sustainable Mountain Agriculture Center located in Berea, KY, from which Brock just received a shoebox-sized shipment of beans, including the Bertie Best. Named after the Aunt Bertie of Dr. Bill Best, president of the organization and perhaps the country's expert on heirloom bean varieties, the Bertie Best Greasy can be white, tan, or black. Bill Best respects his ancestors' decision to never separate out the different colors, and to let nature and the normal pollination process decide what each pod will hold.

GREASY GOOSE BEAN

The Greasy Goose is the result of an accidental hybridization in Brock's field between a Greasy bean and his grandmother's Wild Goose bean. "We were hulling peas that looked white, and then this brownish-red bean popped up." At first, Brock was scared that he'd made a mistake in planting, but then he realized that beans "just work like that," and that he'd created his own bean varietal from his grandmother's favorite beans—another story to add to his family's growing tradition.

DIXIE LEE PEA

The Dixie Lee pea isn't rare, but historically it's been important as a cover crop in the region's seventeen-year crop rotation cycle—a practice that's been replaced with monoculture farming. Brock feels that the first step in reclaiming healthy agricultural practices of the last century is to examine the eating practices that accompanied them. He relies on experts and compatriots like Dr. David Shields of the University of South Carolina to search archival texts for what was on the southern table two centuries back. Brock says, "We have this farm-to-table thing backwards. You first have to understand what was at the table to understand what was going on. These things were grown here because they would thrive."

RED RIPPER PEA

Brock says that eating the Red Ripper is "like eating dirt." And when that's the case, the health of your dirt is important. The more time Brock spends in the field, the more he's come to appreciate the importance of dirt. "The soil is poisoned, there's no nutrients in it," he says. "This pea could be delicious, but if we're growing it in soil that is filled full of industrial and chemical poisons, then there's no nutrient value. So, eventually, it won't matter what we're planting, because it won't have any nutrition. That's what the conversation needs to be about—soil health."

AFRICAN GUINEA CORN

Originating in New England, this variety is an example of the necessity of healthy soil and sound agricultural practices—things that fed the nation before modern technological progress. After hitching a ride on a slave ship from America to Africa, the variety spent 100 years there, growing in nitrogen-rich, nutritious soil. Then it found its way back to America and the low country. A century earlier in New England, the seed would yield one or two ears per stalk—upon its return, it now gives four or five. 🅛🅟

LOSING GROUND

by Sarah Laskow   illustrations by JooHee Yoon

"CURSED IS THE GROUND BECAUSE OF YOU,"
GOD TOLD ADAM. "IN TOIL YOU SHALL EAT
OF IT ALL THE DAYS OF YOUR LIFE."

Plato worried about erosion. So did George Washington. The worry is both ancient and legitimate: farming involves laying fertile topsoil bare, exposed to wind and water, to erode away faster than the earth can generate more.

Today, if you're looking to have a dire conversation about soil, a good person to talk to is David R. Montgomery, a geomorphologist and professor at the University of Washington in Seattle, who plays in a neo-psychedelic alt-folk revival band called Big Dirt and won a Mac-Arthur "genius" grant in 2008. "If you look globally, we don't have enough food at any one time to feed ourselves for a whole year. We're eating hand to mouth," Montgomery says. "That's not a recipe for stability. If something goes wrong—food apocalypse."

The apocalypse that he's talking about—which history shows we all should be worried about—is the one that comes from the erosion of farmland. An underappreciated wonder, soil is a layered terrine of disintegrating rock and decayed organic matter, populated by worms, roots, burrowing animals, and billions of microbes. "It's the most complex biomaterial on Earth," says Ray Weil, a University of Maryland professor who studies soil and sustainable agriculture. "It's filled with far more living things than there are aboveground. They're just small and hard to see." This underground community eats and secretes its way through the soil, breaking down organic and mineral matter into fertile ground. From soil's bottommost layer, where the thick bedrock of the Earth's crust begins crumbling into smaller particles, through the middle layer of hard subsoil and to the rich topsoil, each stratum contains more organic material and potential for fertility than the last. "Even if the soil is fairly thick, the very best soil is at the surface," says Weil, "and that is what erosion takes first."

In wet climates, without plants acting as an umbrella, heavy rain can run across the ground, taking the topsoil with it in sheets of muddy water. In arid places, the topsoil dries out, and the wind carries it away. The richest layer of dirt disappears, and farmers are left to grow crops in less fertile subsoil or with nothing but bedrock. Heavy agricultural use can also drain soil of its fertility, if farmers don't let fields rest and recover; intense irrigation can deposit an overabundance of minerals in the soil, turning it salty and unproductive. The complex, living soil system turns into a crusty skin of dead dirt. Yields drop and people go hungry. Hungry people fight one another for food, move elsewhere, or die out.

This is the future we're rushing toward, at a pace that seems safely slow to an average human, but terrifyingly fast to a geologist. The thickest layers of topsoil are only twelve to sixteen inches deep. It can take 500 years or more to produce an inch of soil, but erosion can remove an inch in a decade. A 2004 analysis from the University of Michigan found that in the eons before humans arrived, soil eroded at a rate of about sixty feet per one million years. In the contemporary United States, agricultural land is eroding twenty-five times that fast. Montgomery likes to compare the world's supply of soil to a savings account. "If

you spend money faster than you make it, you're going broke. It's just a matter of time until you spend through your savings. Soil is exactly the same," he says. "If we run down the supply of fertile land, we're really screwed."

It's happened before. In *Dirt: The Erosion of Civilizations*, Montgomery documented how catastrophic soil mismanagement humbled ancient Greece and Rome. While lifeless soil may not be solely responsible for the downfall of these empires, Montgomery argues that it left them vulnerable to unrest and military conquest. By the time of the Peloponnesian War—about 500 years after city-states like Athens and Sparta began forming—as much as three-quarters of the food supply for Greek cities came from Egypt and Sicily. In the dialogue *Critias,* Plato described how hillsides that had once supported trees now supported only bees, how "the rich, soft soil has all run away leaving the land nothing but skin and bone," and how "an annual rainfall … did not run to waste off the bare earth as it does today." Rome began with an even greater wealth of fertile soil, but five centuries after the founding of the republic, patches of farmland that had once easily supported families were producing only a fraction of what they previously had. Like Greece, the city of Rome became depen-dent on

Egypt and North Africa to feed its population.

Here in America, we've already had one brush with a soil apocalypse. Farmers like Washington documented and worried about erosion, but by the early twentieth century, government officials—under the impression the country's soil would last forever—encouraged farmers to plow up land once thought unfit for agriculture. "The soil is the one indestructible, immutable asset that the Nation possesses," Milton Whitney, who headed the Bureau of Soils, wrote in 1909. "It is the one resource that cannot be exhausted; that cannot be used up."

Whitney had an employee who disagreed: Big Hugh Bennett. The son of a cotton grower, Bennett had an epiphany in the woods of central Virginia early in his career. He and a colleague came across two pieces of land, side by side, that had once been identical. One had never been farmed. The second had been "cropped a long time." The untouched land "was mellow, loamy, and moist enough even in dry weather to dig into with our bare hands." The other strip "was clay, hard, and almost like a rock in dry weather." In 1928, Bennett published a pamphlet called "Soil Erosion: A National Menace."

Two years later, the first notable storm of the Dust Bowl years trawled across the country's High Plains in a cloud of darkness.

Prairie grass had anchored the soil against the winds of the plains, but once farmers plowed through the grass, and drought hit, wind swept away the dry soil in clouds that could grow to more than a mile tall, burying fences, cars, and houses as they passed.

Over the decades, the United States has managed to reverse the damage done during this period—one of the worst examples of soil erosion in history. Experts at the time estimated that in 1935 alone, 850 million tons of topsoil blew off the Southern Plains. That year,

the government formed the Soil Conservation Service (which Bennett headed) and started researching techniques to fight erosion and encouraging farmers to adopt them. Producing a pound of corn in the plains of Iowa can still lead to three or four pounds of soil loss, but compared to the rest of the world, "by and large, the Midwest and

Great Plains have been a success story," says Rattan Lal, professor of soil science at Ohio State University, who's worked on soil issues across the world. A 2006 Cornell University study found that while the United States was losing soil ten times faster than the Earth could provide it, China's soil was eroding three or four times faster than that. Soil scientists predict the worst damage in particularly steep or dry places: the West African Sahel, Haiti, Madagascar, the Himalayan regions.

In the past, farmers saddled with eroded land could move to a new patch of ground. Now, humans have already converted a huge percentage of the Earth's surface to agricultural land. A 1990 study found that over the past 10,000 years more productive soil has been lost than is now being farmed. But even with 38 percent of the planet's land currently under cultivation, complete soil loss is not inevitable. Since the 1960s, scientists like Lal and Weil have been studying no-till farming, which, in its most environmentally responsible form, involves planting without turning the soil first and growing cover crops to protect the soil during fallow periods.

But soil loss happens like hair loss—so slowly that no one quite notices, until one day the field is almost bald. And so farmers make short-term choices and investments. "When people are poor and desperate and starving, they pass on their misery to the land," says Lal. "Stewardship doesn't mean anything to a hungry stomach."

One of the most ambitious ideas for fighting erosion is to change the types of plants we depend on for food altogether. In Salina, Kansas, on the edge of the territory hardest hit in the Dust Bowl, Wes Jackson has been working for thirty years to develop an agricultural system as stable as the ecosystem of prairie grasses that already thrives there. At the Land Institute, Jackson is growing a mix of annual grasses and perennials, which, unlike the wheat and corn farmers grow now, do not need to be planted in the bare earth each year. "There are others that have worked with perennials, but mostly on the side. There's never been a place totally dedicated to perennials," he says. "Where I began is that all of nature's ecosystems feature perennials in mixtures." The Land Institute is working on familiar crops—wheat, rice, sunflower seeds—but crossbreeding annual strains with perennial ones. Eventually the Land Institute wants to see grain growers around the world developing varieties of these perennials that thrive in their particular climates. "If you don't have perennial roots, you're going to have soil erosion," says Jackson. "That's why we say that this is a global concept. It's fit for the whole planet."

Jackson is working against the current of centuries of agricultural practice. Humans have been tinkering— and, recently, genetically engineering—our annual staple crops for ages. Perennials haven't been bred to produce the sort of fat, juicy seeds that make for cheap human sustenance. The work of the Land Institute is to increase the yield of perennials to match that of the crops we grow now. In an ideal future, Big Hugh Bennett wouldn't be able to tell the difference between a wild field and a cultivated one. "Let's say you got a fence and on one side you have native prairie, and on the other, you have our polyculture for grain," says Jackson. "The only difference between the two: the prairie is not producing a large tonnage of seeds"—to be cooked in a pot or ground into flour, baked into bread and made into food. "And the agriculture is."

It'll take years still before the Land Institute's crops will be productive enough for farmers to grow and harvest them commercially. But the researchers are making progress: they've domesticated a perennial strain of wheatgrass, which they call Kernza, and the seeds the plants produce keep getting bigger. From time to time, it's possible, when there are leftovers from seed and milling trials, to buy Kernza flour.

"The yields will be there, but it'll take a long time," Jackson says. "I'm glad we started when we did." **LP**

EPIDEMIOLOGIST (AND MOTHER)

PAT KLUDT, MASSACHUSETTS DEPARTMENT OF PUBLIC HEALTH

Amanda Kludt: What are the most common food-borne illnesses?

Illnesses from salmonella and campylobacter are probably the biggest by volume. Most chicken you purchase in the supermarket has one or both of these bugs. We also follow Listeria and toxin-producing bugs like E. coli O157:H7—the "raw hamburger" bug. Listeria is a more dangerous organism but it's not something that attacks everyone equally.

Anything can spread widely in our present way of distributing food. It's dangerous when our food is produced for mass distribution in one spot. If a single field is contaminated, then you have a whole lot of things contaminated and that spreads across the country. We see it more and more now. In the past we were never able to

put cases together, but now we can look at the DNA of the organism and we get together and find the common thread.

Are vegetables as dangerous as meat?

Everything has its risk. As a whole, the food in the United States is really very safe, but there can be large countrywide outbreaks. We found salmonella in peanut butter. The peanut butter went into jars of peanut butter, crackers, cookies, and ice cream, among other products. There were just so many places this peanut butter went. It was very difficult to find out what everyone ate to get us back to the plant.

If people wash their fruit, will they be okay?

We found that people are less likely to become ill if they at least rinse their produce. Think about a watermelon. You get a whole

INTERVIEW BY AMANDA KLUDT
ILLUSTRATIONS BY JING WEI

watermelon, and you just bring it home from the store, and you slice into it. But you've now sliced whatever was on the outside of the watermelon into the inside.

If I pick up a container of blackberries in February, they're coming from Ecuador or Guatemala. You wouldn't eat those berries unwashed if you were in Guatemala or Ecuador, right? You would try to wash them; you would try to sanitize them in some way.

As an epidemiologist and my mom, what were some things you forbade my sister and me from eating as kids?

I didn't come to this job until you were eight and Megan was twelve, so until then I had no idea, and that's still a problem we face now—people having no idea. The first case of Shiga toxin-producing E. coli in burgers wasn't even identified as a food problem until 1982, so it's quite new. When I started the job in 1992 it was well established as a pathogen, and that was the end of pink burgers for you and for me. The Northeast had also just recently begun seeing salmonella in eggs. That was the end of runny eggs for us.

The E. colis that produce toxins can be especially bad in children. There are a number of them now besides E. coli O157. There was a large outbreak in 2011 that affected many countries, starting with Germany. It came with bean sprouts. But E. coli O157, which is found in the intestines of cattle, is still the most common. Slaughtering cattle is not a very clean process and meat

can become contaminated from the intestines. That's why we always want people to cook their hamburgers all the way through, especially for kids: they are the most at risk for deadly complications. If you're going to eat a raw hamburger, fine, just don't feed it to your kids. Make their burgers well done. With a steak, theoretically since it's a slice of meat, any organisms from the intestines or outside of the meat won't reach the inside of the steak. You can broil the top and the bottom, and you'll be okay. But when you grind up meat for hamburger, it's all mixed up—any contamination from the slaughter is going to be on the inside of the hamburger and on the outside. So you really want to treat that hamburger as if it's full of contaminants.

What are the big things people need to do to avoid getting sick?

They need to cook most foods thoroughly, follow the directions on the packages, wash their hands.

We had an outbreak of E. coli O157 in raw cookie dough. You're supposed to cook it before you eat it, so manufacturers don't include a step to kill bacteria in production. No particular ingredient was a potentially hazardous food. But something got contaminated. And because there wasn't that kill step, people got sick. It was interesting to see how many people ate it raw—a lot.

Another thing we're seeing is that people don't know the wattage of their microwaves. The instructions on microwavable dinners are for a particular wattage. Microwaves vary from model to model, and can range from about 300 watts to 1000 watts or more. People blindly following instructions may not realize they have microwaves with a wattage lower than the instructions specify. These people may not cook things long enough, to a safe internal temperature.

There are certain things I prefer not to eat. One in ten thousand eggs are contaminated with salmonella. I've had no problems ordering two eggs over easy, because what are my chances that one of those is the one in ten thousand? But, at a restaurant where they start cracking and beating eggs together at the beginning of a shift, your chances increase of getting that contaminated egg. If I'm making angel food cake with ten to twelve eggs, I'm not going to let you lick the beater.

People who like drinking raw milk and eating rare burgers—are there any precautions they can take while still enjoying the thing they want?

Just know your farm. Know where it's coming from. Feel comfortable with your food source. If you're going to drink raw milk, go to the farm, talk to the people, trust them. Not that they can always know that their cows don't have salmonella or E. coli, but at least you can feel comfortable that if they do know they have an unhealthy animal, they won't give you that milk.

There are rules in place, because some states allow the sale of raw milk. Massachusetts allows it at the farm. Some states allow it in stores. There are rules about how it gets bottled and sold, but I would feel more comfortable if I could meet my milk producer down the road. And the smaller the herd, the better it's going to be.

We have come a long way with milk to make sure it's safe, mostly because of pasteurization. There are other opinions, and we respect those other opinions, but our opinion is that pasteurization prevents the spread of pathogens through milk.

What can we reasonably do to fix our current system and minimize the risks?

I think people need to be willing to pay more for food. It costs more to operate a cleaner environment. It costs more to regulate the food industry to make sure safe practices are being followed. The federal government needs to be more efficient when it comes to overseeing the food supply. Right now, the USDA oversees some things, the FDA others, and the interaction between the two does not always go smoothly. They only discovered the peanut-butter outbreak because there was an outbreak. The system is reactive and not proactive.

What are you worried about in general in terms of food safety? Where are we headed?

I am worried where the next outbreak is going to come from. It's already showing up where we never expected: snack foods, peanut butter, leafy greens, cookie dough, tomatoes, peppers, cheese, apple cider, orange juice, berries, oysters. We can make a lot of people sick from just being stupid, careless, cheap, and greedy. Ⓛ

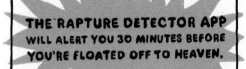

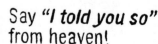

PASTAPOCALYPSE

On day three of the blackout/flood in New York caused by Hurricane Sandy, I went to the bodega, and the only things they had on the shelf were dog food and Chef Boyardee.

I almost chose the dog food. But it had been a long time since I'd tasted the Chef's cooking, so I went for the red can. When I got it home, I was crestfallen when I realized I don't even own a can opener. Thankfully, the can had one of those pull-tab easy-open things installed on top! That's an invention on par with Velcro.

As I sat there hunkered down with my pasta, I thought, Man, we should see what an Italian food expert thinks about this stuff. Mark Ladner, the chef of Del Posto, is one of the best chefs in America and an authority on Italian cooking, though clearly a man of poor judgement as he accepted my invitation.

The parameters of our little experiment were that it's the end of the world, and we've gone underground. There are no more fresh tomatoes—there's nothing. No heat. No silverware, just sporks. (I think that people should embrace the spork: it's America's chopstick!) Straight out of the can into a bowl is the only way to eat. See some of our tasting notes below.

After being repulsed by our findings, Mark demonstrated that pasta can be made from shelf-stable ingredients and not taste like, well... let's just say that after our experiment, the next few times I see Mark, drinks are on me.   —**DAVE CHANG**

CHEF BOYARDEE SPAGHETTI AND MEATBALLS

ML: It's actually nicely sauced. But it's really unbelievable how overcooked the noodles are. They're still intact, but they don't require any teeth.

DC: I ate this as a kid. Why it happened, I don't remember. But I believe that a lot of people eat these.

ML: Does anyone think it's good? Like, they look forward to this? Or is it just sustenance?

ANNIE'S BERNIE O'S

ML: The can says, "Eat with a fork, a spoon, or sandbox shovel. Hot or cold, or hot with an ice cube." Who thinks that shit up?

DC: There's no xanthan gum in here. Cornstarch, though. Organic cheddar—it's all organic.

ML: Chef Boyardee is still kicking ass as far as I'm concerned.

SHOPRITE SCRUNCHY SPAGHETTI RINGS & MINI MEATBALLS

ML: Hmm. A soy meatball... it's really soft.

DC: They're tiny ones. I feel like this would be a big reward in prison.

ML: The pasta is just so flaccid. It's fucking annihilated. Let's call original Chef Boyardee the winner and be done with this.

CHEF BOYARDEE CHEESYBURGER MACARONI

ML: This is interesting. Cheesyburger macaroni. This must be a more modern development.

DC: I don't know if I can eat this. [Tastes] Wow. It's totally, utterly, disgustingly flavorless. I think I would rather eat a human being. You know who might like this? Wylie Dufresne.

CALAMARATA ALLA BOSCAIOLO

Rigatoni with tomatoes, porcini, and tuna | *Makes 4 to 6 servings*

Rehydrate porcinis ⟶ Cook sauce ⟶ Boil pasta ⟶ Combine; serve

Twice I've cooked with a woman named Paulo di Mauro in Marino, outside of Rome, where the Pope's summer home is. She's supposed to be the leading authority on classical Roman cuisine and both times she was cooking directly out of *The Food of Rome and Lazio* by Oretta Zanini de Vita. So the book is legit, and I can confirm that it's awesome—I use it all the time. It's where I picked out the idea for this pasta.

This pasta would be fine with ordinary Italian ingre-dients, but I've spent years finding and squirreling away high-quality shelf-stable ingredients, like Sicilian tomato paste—it's intensely flavorful and solid like clay—and the $30-a-jar Sicilian tuna belly I used to make this recipe. My advice is to get out there, find this stuff, and lay some down in the pantry before the end of the world, because the better your ingredients, the better your end-times eating will be.

—**MARK LADNER**

INGREDIENTS & EQUIPMENT

1 C	dried porcini mushrooms
+	salt
2 T	olive oil, plus a splash more to finish
2 to 3 T	Sicilian tomato paste
1	12-oz can cherry tomatoes
1-2 T	Calabrian chili pepper condiment
½ C	tuna packed in oil
1 lb	large-diameter rigatoni, or similar dried Italian pasta

1 Combine the porcini with enough water to cover in a sauce pan. Bring to a boil then drop the heat to a simmer and cook until the porcini are tender—about 20 to 30 minutes.

2 Drain the porcini, reserving their cooking liquid in the pot you will eventually cook your pasta in. Top off with enough water to cook the pasta. (I don't use gallons of water, just enough to cover the pasta by an inch or two. *See note on page 45.*) Add a large pinch of salt, and put it on the stove to boil.

3 Meanwhile, heat the olive oil in a skillet or sauté pan over medium heat. After a minute, add the tomato paste and cook, stirring occasionally, for 4 to 5 minutes. Add the cherry tomatoes and the liquid they're packed in, the chili condiment, and the drained porcini.

*Cook porcinis until tender, then use the liquid to boil the pasta (**step 2**).*

*Cook the tomatoes and porcini for a few minutes to let the flavors meld (**step 3**).*

Drop the pasta into the boiling water, while you cook the tomatoes and mushrooms for 5 to 10 minutes, just to bring the flavors together.

4 Boil the rigatoni a minute shy of the recommended cooking time, then drain. Add the tuna to the sauce just before you're about to add the pasta. The tuna comes fully cooked in the jar, so you don't want to hammer it or else it'll become really chalky.

5 Add the pasta to the sauce, and cook, tossing and stirring, until the pasta is well-coated in the sauce. Add a splash more oil, toss once again, and serve.

If you're making this before the apocalypse, or if your herb garden has survived unscathed, a bit of chopped fresh parsley would be a welcome addition.

POMPEII PREPPER'S PASTA

Whole-wheat penne with walnuts and anchovies | *Makes 4 to 6 servings*

Start boiling pasta → Make sauce → Combine → Garnish and serve

This is a shelf-stable, dairy-free pasta for the healthy-ish pescatarian: who knows who you'll end up having to cook for down in your bunker?

I've used whole-wheat pasta because I like it and because I think it behaves well. And I actually really like De Cecco—I think it's designed intentionally to be over-cooked a bit and still be al dente. I have been to De Cecco Land, to the factory in Italy, but the last time I went they turned me away. There were armed guards! I swear it's like going into the fortress of a James Bond villain—it's out in the middle of fucking nowhere, literally cut out of the side of a mountain. Probably would be a good place to hide out in the end of days.

I've been messing around with coconut oil for cooking—it works well, though it seems to have a relatively low smoke point. In lieu of walnuts, this could be made with canned chickpeas, which are one of my favorite canned products. They're all perfectly cooked; you just need to rinse off the mucous and go. I'd use non-shelf-stable silken tofu in a non-apocalypse situation—it's creamier and tastes better.

I've learned that nutritional yeast is a decent dairy-free stand in for grated cheese, so I used that here. At Del Posto, we get a lot of large group reservations, so we try to get people to do tasting menus. Not really elaborate douchey ones but, like, everybody at the table chooses an appetizer and then the table chooses three pastas and everyone gets the same thirty-gram portion of each pasta. But then you always end up with all these dietary restrictions. Out of ten people, three people will be allergic to shellfish, another gluten intolerant, and the third doesn't want any salt or something. That's where it gets really hard for the kitchen. But it's not fair to penalize the other five people because three people don't want cheese. I'm sure there are plenty of places out there with the same problem with a $25 check average, so I'm not complaining. But a huge part of my job at the restaurant has been learning how to deal with challenges like that, and yeast does the trick in the dairy-free-pasta-that-wants-cheese situation.

I finish with bonito flakes, because—and it's taken me years to admit this—I just like bonito (or *katsuobushi*) better than I like bottarga. —**MARK LADNER**

INGREDIENTS	
+	salt
1 lb	whole-wheat penne
2 T	coconut oil
14	walnuts
2	meaty anchovies, filleted
2 T	capers on the branch, packed in oil
½ box	puréed silken tofu
1 T	nutritional yeast
2 big pinches	bonito flakes

1 **Bring a pot of water to a boil and salt it well.*** Drop the pasta in, and cook it for a minute shy of what the package recommends.

2 **Meanwhile, heat the coconut oil** in a skillet or sauté pan over medium heat. After a minute, add the walnuts and anchovy fillets and cook for 4 to 5 minutes, until the walnuts have begun to take on a smidge of color. Add the capers and half the puréed silken tofu to the pan and stir well. Keep over low heat until the pasta is ready.

3 **Drain the pasta well** and add it to the pan. Stir in the additional tofu, tossing to coat the pasta. Taste and add fresh water to loosen the sauce—between ¼ and ½ C to get the consistency right. What I like to do—just as a general philosophy—is to cook the pasta in heavily salted water so that you really get the salt impact in the pasta itself. Then any additional water I add to the sauce is always fresh. If you add salted water

to sauce with aged cheese or cured pork products that have been rendered (bacon), you can make it too salty. And as the sauce reduces, the salt will intensify, so it's generally much safer to use fresh water.

4 **Turn out the pasta onto serving plates**. Scatter the yeast over the top like it's grated Parmesan cheese, and garnish generously with bonito flakes. Serve immediately.

* **A note on cooking pasta**: I don't usually subscribe to all the rules about how much water to use in cooking pasta. There are people like Alain Ducasse, who cook all their pasta risotto style and it comes out really starchy. It's just a matter of personal preference. I don't like when the surface of the pasta feels starchy. I like the sauce to adhere to the pasta because of the lipids and gelatin in the sauce, rather than natural starch from the pasta, because it feels really tacky on my palate.

Basically, I use enough water to submerge the pasta, then I stir once or twice in the first minute.

You really shouldn't have to worry about it after that unless you just completely packed way too much pasta into the pan. I undercook all dried pastas by 2 to 3 minutes (we time all of our pasta cooking) and finish them in the sauce they'll be served in.

Like I said, I don't subscribe to a lot of rules anymore. When I was younger it was different. Sometimes these really arduous processes that people have done for generations are really a waste of time and not generally appreciated by the diners.

Risotto is an example of a rule I still follow: lots of restaurants get more attention for their risotto than we do. We make our risotto in the most arduous and traditional method. But then again, we charge a lot for it. So while we can afford and do make risotto the "right" old way, I don't begrudge people finding a faster way to a very similar endpoint.

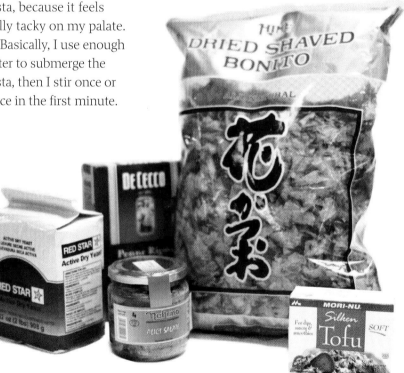

SPAGHETTI ALLA VODKA *Side-by-side taste test*

Honestly, until I was in the supermarket picking up some of the ingredients for this little cooking experiment, I'd never seen Mario Batali or Lidia Bastianich's jarred vodka sauces. And until cooking them, I'd never even had an alla vodka sauce, even though I know it's on, like, every bar and airport Italian menu in the world. But I figure if you're really gonna be in the shits, some canned tomato sauce and spaghetti couldn't hurt to have around, and who better to get it from than my two bosses?

In my informal taste test, I found that Lidia's is fruitier and maybe herbier. Mario's tastes like it's got a little chili in it—maybe it's that vodka sting on the back of the throat. I kind of sense their personalities through their sauces. Mario's is obviously heavier on the cream, which would explain the color, but they're both pretty good and not too dissimilar. In fact I'd probably just mix them together if I were cooking with them.

—**MARK LADNER**

GRANNY PANTRIES

BY ANNE WHEELER

IN 1959 MARIA RODRIGUEZ and Melvin Mininson won a contest. The prize was a two-week honeymoon in an 8' × 14' steel-and-concrete room, buried twelve feet under the yard of a modest ranch-style home in Miami. A fallout shelter.

The couple was promised an actual Mexican honeymoon following the completion of their fallout-shelter stint, but even so, the "prize" seems a bit dubious. But 1959 was the absolute height of the atomic age in America. *Life* magazine noted in an article about the Mininsons, "Fallout can be fun." Fallout shelters were a status symbol, epitomizing the archetype of American invincibility: of course we could overcome anything, even destruction by thermonuclear war.

Across the country, concern was pervasive, and the media sent a measured, practical message of preparation. Complete global annihilation is inevitable, so you better stock up on canned spaghetti.

PLAZA 1-9991
PLAZA 1-2809

CANAL 1-2446

BOMB SHELTERS, INC.
"It Will Save Your Life"

PAUL S. INDIANER
SECY.-TREAS.

1475 N. E. 131ST STREET
NORTH MIAMI, FLORIDA

THE FALLOUT-SHELTER CONTEST WAS put on by a radio station and a bomb-shelter manufacturer (the creatively named Bomb Shelters, Inc., of North Miami) whose motto was "It Will Save Your Life." Conspicuous consumption was the name of the game during the atomic age—the more your family bought, the more anti-communist you were. Capitalism, especially of the defending-the-nuclear-family sort, was patriotism. Food and sanitary science companies lined up to stock their goods in the Mininsons' fallout shelter as "wedding gifts."

THE MININSONS HEADED UNDERGROUND with Carnation powdered milk, peanut butter, canned spaghetti, tuna, stew, and creamed corn among other practical, sensible wedding gifts. However, once underground, the couple was met with a handful of issues. They used Sterno to cook stew, canned spaghetti, and creamed corn, but complained, "There is not enough variety in the foods that are provided, too much stew and tuna, [and] we hardly touched the peanut butter." The bigger issue for the couple was the can opener. Mr. Mininson explained that the can opener was broken, noting that he had to use the scissors from the first aid kit to open the canned provisions, which caused him to slice open his hand, requiring other first-aid tackle to repair the damage. Officials decided that the can opener worked fine, and that the honeymooning couple simply did not know how to use it.

The Conelrad Collection

DEEP IN THE BELLY of the fallout shelter, a pajama-clad, newly minted Mrs. Mininson sits at the fold-out dinette set enjoying a glass of reconstituted Carnation powdered milk and a bowl of uncanned foodstuffs.

THE MININSONS' HONEYMOON FOOD was selected by a specialist at the Federal Civil Defense Administration (FCDA). The FCDA was very good at making lists and guidelines and programs and all sorts of other paperwork for Americans to follow in the face of thermonuclear war

MAINE WAS PARTICULARLY GUNG HO about preparedness, and especially enthusiastic about Grandma's Pantry, one of the FCDA's most prominent programs.

The program relied on carefully segregated gender roles and traditional "American" imagery: an old-timey pot-bellied stove and a well stocked larder straight out of *Little House on the Prairie.*

GRANDMA'S PANTRY WAS READY

Federal Civil Defense Administration

Is Your "Pantry" Ready in Event of Emergency?

THE PROGRAM HAD AS many tote bags as your local NPR station. Cardboard displays were rolled out for county fairs and department-store windows. Civil defense volunteers passed out scads of literature. The basic brochure was a wonderfully fuzzy, purple-blue-inked mimeographed leaflet customized to local tastes.

Maine Historical Society

U.S. Government Printing Office

GRANDMA'S PANTRY BROCHURES OUTLINED the approximate portions required for an individual for fallout shelter stays of three, seven, or fourteen days (the supposed time it would take for an all-clear for radioactive fallout).

Two methods were suggested for water storage. One was to can your stock water in mason jars "like the women in Utah do." The other was to finish a bottle of Clorox and fill the jug with tap water, recap it, and move it underground. The leftover chlorine in the bottle would be enough to purify the water for shelter stays of any length.

MAINE OFFERED A MEMBERSHIP card to housewives with adequately stocked pantries. The idea was to gather the items ringing the card, and sign it certifying that you had done your wifely part in securing your family's postapocalyptic future.

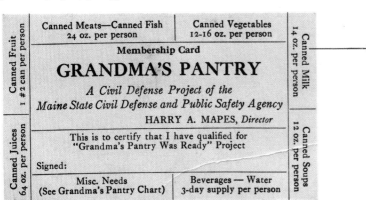

Canned Meats—Canned Fish
24 oz. per person

Canned Vegetables
12–16 oz. per person

Canned Fruit
1 # 2 can per person

Canned Milk
14 oz. per person

Membership Card

GRANDMA'S PANTRY

A Civil Defense Project of the
Maine State Civil Defense and Public Safety Agency

HARRY A. MAPES, *Director*

This is to certify that I have qualified for
"Grandma's Pantry Was Ready" Project

Signed:

Canned Juices
64 oz. per person

Canned Soups
12 oz. per person

Misc. Needs
(See Grandma's Pantry Chart)

Beverages — Water
3-day supply per person

Grandma's Pantry Returns
As Civil Defense Factor

By MARIANNE KELSEY
Times Staff Writer

FCDA Urges 7-Day Emergency
Food Supply for All Families

LISTS WERE PRINTED IN various newspapers across the nation. In one list, the *Naples Record* included two types of milk yet the very broad categories of "soups" and "vegetables." The *St. Petersburg Times* was curiously specific with three different types of canned milk, chowders, and string beans.

CIVIL DEFENSE FALLOUT SHELTER CHECK LIST

COMPLIMENTS OF

THE WALLACE CEILINGS & SOUND CONDITIONING CO.

AT 2-5580

SHELTER CHECKLIST

Food and cooking equipment:
Water (2-week supply, a minimum of 7 gal. per person)
Food (2-week supply)
Eating utensils
Paper plates, cups, and napkins (2-week supply)
Openers for cans and bottles
Pocket knife
Special foods for babies and the sick

Supplies and equipment for sanitation:
Can for garbage (20-gal.)
Covered pail for toilet purposes
Can for human wastes (10-gal.)
Toilet tissue, paper towels, sanitary napkins, disposable diapers, ordinary and waterless soap
Grocery bags, newspapers for soil bags
Household chlorine (2 pt.) and DDT (1 qt. of 5% solution)
Waterproof gloves

Shelter equipment:
Battery radio with CONELRAD frequencies (640 or 1240) marked, and spare batteries for 2-week operation
Home-use radiation instruments
Flashlights, electric lantern, and spare batteries for 2 weeks
Clothing
Bedding (rubber sheeting and special equipment for the sick)
A first-aid kit and supplies listed in OCDM Leaflet L-2-12, *First Aid: Emergency Kit; Emergency Action*
Writing material
Reading material
Screwdriver, pliers, and other household tools
Games and amusements for children

Items outside the shelter but within reach:
Cooking equipment (canned heat, or camp stove) and matches
Home fire-fighting equipment
Rescue tools

MAIL TO:
WALLACE
P. O. BOX 4526
RICHMOND 29, VA.

FALLOUT SHELTERS

Since there is no obligation, please call on me to talk over plans and ideas.

NAME
ADDRESS
PHONE

PROVIDING EMERGENCY-PREPAREDNESS CHECKLISTS BECAME a common courtesy. Here, an acoustic tile manufacturer jumped on the bandwagon.

FOR LAZIER TYPES, GENERAL MILLS was there to help out. General Mills developed a granular protein mix called Multi-Purpose Food (MPF) that could be eaten "hot or cold, wet or dry." Three scoops of MPF met the daily food needs of your average 1950s American. For taste's sake, it was recommended that the diner blend MPF with other foods like peanut butter. **LP**

PECAN PRALINELLA

Bomb shelter essential | Makes 1½ pints

Make praline pecans → Purée pecan butter → Make ganache → Combine and can → Serve or Store

I didn't discover Nutella until my early twenties, when my sister's Italian boyfriend fed me a nutty-chocolaty goo-slathered slice of toast that dropped a megaton bomb on a whole swath of my childhood memories. All those years I spent eating PB&J when I could've been eating Nutella!

Eventually, after extensive electroshock therapy, I regained my composure. Today I'm well enough to offer you this Pralinella—a homemakable version of Nutella-like goodness. It's made with pecans instead of hazelnuts in honor of one of my few remaining happy memories of growing up in the great state of Texas: the individually-wrapped candied pecans next to the cash registers in Austin's finer Tex-Mex restaurants. I've also swapped out the regular chocolate for white. I have an active dislike for plain white chocolate, but when it's toasted it takes on a caramel-y, nutty, brown-buttery flavor that I can't get enough of. A dash of cayenne adds zing; pimentón adds a hint of smoke; miso anchors the spread with a deep salty/umami note.

It tastes delicious spread on toast, or as a dip for apples. I understand that after the apocalypse, your toast and apple selection might be slim. Well, if you have to resort to eating garbage, you may as well slather it with praline deliciousness. So add a jar to your emergency stockpile of whiskey, batteries, canned meat, and trashy romance novels. This lasts a long time in the fridge, and it'll hold on the shelf for at least a month or two. —**COURTNEY MCBROOM**

INGREDIENTS & EQUIPMENT

2 C	pecans
½ C	maple syrup
1 t	kosher salt
Scant ⅛ t	cayenne

WHITE-CHOCOLATE GANACHE

1 C + ½ C	Valrhona white chocolate, coarsely chopped
⅓ C	light corn syrup
1¼ t	white (shiro) miso
1 t	kosher salt
2 T + 1 t	light brown sugar
⅛ t	smoked paprika
1⅓ C	heavy cream

1 Preheat the oven to 325°F.
Combine the praline ingredients in a mixing bowl, and toss thoroughly.

2 Transfer the pecans to a parchment-lined baking sheet and roast for 20 to 25 minutes. Halfway through the baking process, pull out the sheet and stir everything around.

*Cooking times may vary for the pecans. Roast until they're mahogany (**step 2**).*

You're looking for the nuts to turn dark without being burnt. The darker the nut, the better the flavor: mahogany is the color you want.

3 Remove nuts from the oven and let them cool for 5 minutes, then grind them in a food processor until they break down into a smooth butter—this will take several minutes of pulsing and processing. Set aside 1 C of praline butter. Eat any extra.

5 Make the white-chocolate ganache: Combine 1 C white chocolate with the rest of the ingredients—except the heavy cream—in a small saucepan. Heat over medium-low heat, stirring constantly with a heat-proof spatula.

6 Once the chocolate melts, turn the heat up to medium and continue to cook, stirring constantly, to caramelize the chocolate. Once the mixture becomes a shade darker than miso, remove it from the heat and slowly whisk in the heavy cream and unmelted white chocolate.

7 While the chocolate mixture is still warm, marry it with 1 C pecan butter in a mixing bowl or the pan you cooked the choclate in. Whisk until the two become one.

If you intend to eat the pralinella soon, chill it overnight in an airtight container. For improved shelf stability, sanitize a glass jar with boiling water, fill with pralinella, seal, submerge in boiling water, and boil for 20 minutes. If the product separates, shake it until it comes back together.

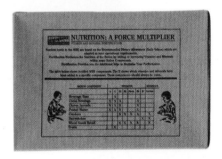

Materials Resembling Edibles

BY JOY Y. WANG

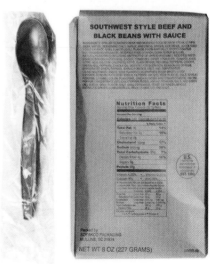

Should the world suddenly succumb to zombie plague or nuclear winter, one might consider spending one's precious final fumes of gasoline heading toward Asheville, North Carolina. There, in the heart of the Appalachians' bastion of tie-dyed liberalism, lies the MRE Logistics warehouse and approximately 125,000 meals ready to eat.

The origins of the MRE can be traced back to Napoleon's declaration that "an army marches on its stomach." In 1795, he offered 12,000 francs as a reward to anyone who could prevent rations from spoiling: hunger and food-supply issues were bogging his troops down as much as combat itself. The French military

PHOTOS BY CHRIS YING

had been relying on age-old means of food preservation—pickling, fermenting, salting, drying, and smoking—that did not always prevent the food from going bad.

Fifteen years after Napoleon first issued the challenge, French chef Nicolas Appert claimed the reward: he discovered that by stuffing meat into a bottle, sealing it, and boiling the whole thing, the food could be held at ambient temperature without going bad. Using that method, he was also able to preserve soups, vegetables, fruits, and dairy products. The French navy bought his glass-jarred goods in 1806 and attested that the food kept for long periods of time without spoiling. Appert's 1810 paper titled "The Art of Preserving All Kinds of Animal and Vegetable Substances for Several Years" won him the prize money, which he used to open the world's first cannery in Massy, France. Thus the precursor of the modern-day MRE was born.

A little more than fifty years later, though, most Civil War soldiers in America were not yet benefiting from Appert's discovery. While canned goods were available, they were expensive and difficult to transport. Instead, Union and Confederate soldiers mostly survived on hardtack (or "sheet-iron crackers," made from flour, salt, and water), cornmeal, and salted meat. When possible, troops also traveled with cattle and ate vegetables that were shredded, dried, and pressed into clumps. The desiccated vegetables were commonly referred to as "desecrated vegetables," and one soldier in the Third Iowa cavalry regiment declared, "We have

boiled, baked, fried, stewed, pickled, sweetened, salted it; tried it in puddings cakes and pies; but it sets all modes of cooking in defiance, so the boys break it up and smoke it in their pipes!"

By World War I, canned rations (C rations) had taken the place of hardtack and salted bacon. Instead of the glass jars initially used by Appert, soldiers hauled tins of sardines, salmon, and beef, as well as hard bread, coffee, salt, and sugar. During World War II, troops ate monotonous diets of similar C rations, though paratroopers under assault conditions were given K rations, which were pocket-size meals that included items like cigarettes, bouillon cubes, canned meat product, and canned cheese product. During the war, soldiers coined the nickname "shit on a shingle" to refer to a ubiquitous dish of canned creamed chipped beef on toast.

C rations were rebranded as "meal, combat, individual" (MCI) during the Cold War era, when the military began focusing on providing nutritionally balanced meals. MCIs came in the form of twelve menus that averaged 1,200 calories apiece. By the time of the Vietnam War, MCIs were still considered the general-purpose ration, but advancements in processing and packaging led to the creation of long-range patrol rations: freeze-dried meals like chicken and rice, spaghetti, and escalloped potatoes.

It was around this time that the military began developing meals ready to eat as we know them today. The goal was to get rid of the metal cans and start packing food in strong, flexible, multilayer pouches.

The first MRE in such a pouch was sent into the field in 1983.

These days, MREs are sealed in four-layer laminate pouches made from high-barrier polymers that keep out light, moisture, and oxygen—packaging that has been co-opted for commercial tuna.

"Flexible packaging found its first use in the MREs of the early eighties," says Jeannette Kennedy, a senior food technologist at the US Army Natick Soldier Research, Development, and Engineering Center outside of Boston. "The military is a driver for a lot of the stuff that you see on the grocery store shelf, such as a lot of the freeze-dried technology used in coffee, or Kool-Aid."

Kennedy is charged with improving MREs, and she says that the military creates today's MREs using the same process that Appert developed more than 200 years ago.

"The MRE entrée items are thermal sterilized," Kennedy says. "The MRE pouches basically go in a big pressure cooker." The squishy laminate packets of chicken with noodles, maple sausage, and vegetable lasagna are heated to a high enough temperature to zap all the germs. That temperature varies depending on the food, but microbial kill tends to happen around 240°F. The military now offers twenty-four different entrées. Since 1990 they've added more than 261 new individual items.

While the food scientists and engineers at Natick develop the specifications for MREs, the meals are primarily made by and purchased from three commercial companies: AmeriQual Group, SOPAKCO, and The Wornick Company. MRE Logistics, a smaller company, sells 1.5 million MREs with about eleven different menus every year. The military buys approximately half of that total; civilian purchases account for the rest.

The downside of thermal sterilization is that high heat invariably affects the taste, texture, and appearance of the food. It's already cooked when it's heated again in what's referred to as "the retort process" to achieve shelf-stable sterilization. Warfighters (which is what the military calls soldiers now) refer to the resulting taste as retort flavor.

"It's like a potted-meat flavor," Kennedy explains. "The retort flavor is a dulling of the flavor profile."

Maintaining color, texture, and general recognizability also presents a hurdle to the retort process. Ken Lester, the director of sales at MRE Logistics, admits that the company avoids creating anything with eggs or potatoes. Once retorted, eggs "don't look exactly like the eggs you order from the restaurant," he says. "Potatoes don't come out exactly the color you expect." For pasta, the company only uses thicker noodles like penne, which are able to stand up to the heat without disintegrating to mush.

"The other major disadvantage to thermo-sterilizing is that some nutrients essentially get cooked out of the food," Kennedy adds. "We end up fortifying different products with vitamins and nutrients to make sure [warfighters are] getting proper nutrition."

Lauren Oleksyk, the head of the Food Processing, Engineering, and Technology team at Natick, is charged with the task of finding ways to improve the flavor of MREs, and purge them of their canned, overcooked taste. Much of the cutting-edge research and development she oversees is geared toward the goal of preserving freshness and nutrients. Once Oleksyk develops an acceptable process, she works to get FDA approval before the commercial companies start using the technology.

Recently the military and its contractors have been employing microwave sterilization. The advantage is that food doesn't need to be heated for as long as with traditional thermal sterilization, which uses steam and pressure to reach safe temperatures. Using microwaves means better taste, color, texture, and nutrient retention. A cut of beef, for instance, would need only eight minutes in the microwave sterilizer, as opposed to nearly an hour in a thermal sterilizer.

Oleksyk says that microwave sterilization has been the biggest leap in technology since Appert started canning two centuries ago. Though microwave ovens have been used in households since the 1970s, the FDA has only recently approved the use of microwave technology for food sterilization. "That process alone is going to change the food industry," Oleksyk says. "We're getting approval left and right from the FDA for it. That's something I'm really excited about, because within a year, you're going to see shelf-stable food on grocery store shelves that you won't even know is microwave sterilized."

Oleksyk and her team are also looking once again to France for ideas. In particular, they're experimenting with osmotic dehydration, which is a technology currently being used by a research and development institute supported by the French meat industry. The process increases the shelf life of meat products like prosciutto and ham.

Here's what happens: ground meat is spread between two layers of parchment paper and flattened. The flattened meat is then sent through a solution that is 75 percent maltitol syrup and 25 percent water. Water naturally moves from the meat into the solution, where the osmotic pressure is higher. The process dries the meat, but it doesn't change its taste. Finally, the meat is quickly blasted with heat to kill off microbes.

A widespread hope in the industry is that all these advances in technology will one day lead to the holy grail of MREs: pizza. Pizza is the military's most requested but most elusive, hardest to produce menu item.

Combining crust, sauce, cheese, and toppings in a shelf-stable package poses all manner of problems. Too much moisture and the pizza will be soggy or, worse, spoil. Too little moisture, and you don't really have pizza.

"We're looking at putting in laminate between the layers," Oleksyk tells me excitedly. "It'd be edible transparent films that you wouldn't see. When you go to consume the pizza, you wouldn't taste it."

One chilly Thursday night, I ripped open an MRE pouch that Natick sent to my Brooklyn apartment labeled "Southwest beef and black beans." Out spilled four smaller dirt-brown packages: raspberry-flavored sugar-free beverage powder, picante sauce and chunky peanut butter in separate oversize condiment packets, and shrink-wrapped crackers on which to spread the peanut butter. Three flat cardboard boxes held pouches labeled "beef stew," "mexican rice and beans," and "apple pieces in spiced sauce." A small clear plastic bag contained salt, ground red pepper, sugar, creamer, napkins, gum, matches, instant coffee, dirt-brown plastic utensils, and a moist towelette. Finally, there was a plastic, resealable beverage bag for mixing powdered drinks, a flameless ration heater—a frosted-plastic bag containing a pad with a mixture of magnesium and iron and salt—and detailed instructions on how to heat everything up.

As instructed, I added a few tablespoons of water up to a line about an inch from the bottom of the flameless ration heater bag. Immediately, the reaction between water and the heating element produced a sickly waft of smoke that smelled like a short circuit of plastic-coated wiring. I dropped the packet of stew into the heater bag, then carefully stuffed it all into the cardboard box. The directions said to lean one end of the box against a "rock or something" at a 45-degree angle. I marveled at how quickly heat began emanating from the box. Kennedy had explained that the flameless ration heater is able to heat food 100°F above ambient temperature.

After about five minutes, I fished the packet out of the box and replaced it with the rice and beans, then the spiced apple pieces. I ripped the top off the stew packet and dug into the pouch with a plastic fork. The stew was warm, if not actually hot. It tasted like something I'd expect from a commercial soup brand—salty and somewhat squishy. The rice could have used more time in the heater, as the grains were still on the al dente side when I pulled it out, but once I mixed it in with the stew, the resulting combo was fairly palatable. The apple pieces in the cinnamon-flavored sauce were tasty and completely normal—particularly after I spooned them over some vanilla ice cream from my freezer and crumbled an M&M cookie on top.

The cookie came from another MRE packet Natick sent with cheese tortellini, a "first strike" energy bar, cheese spread, crackers, M&Ms, instant spiced cider, and an assortment of other odds and ends. After being warmed up in a flameless ration heater, the tortellini tasted like commercially available canned pasta—which means I'd have happily eaten it in younger, drunker days.

Servicemen and -women who aren't so foolish as to consume MREs just for fun have adapted to the reality of surviving on the stuff in the field. If there's a way to make shelf-stable food more enjoyable, chances are a soldier's tried it.

"What I remember the most was the chemical cardboard slip," says former Army Carpentry Masonry Specialist Ann Treadaway, referring to the magnesium-and-iron pad in the flameless ration heater. "The smell from that made it very unappetizing." Treadaway, who served in the Army Corps of Engineers and was deployed to Iraq twice, frequently opted to eat her MREs cold.

Treadaway says she never noticed anyone eat the jalapeño cheese spread in their MREs, but former Navy Information System Technician, Petty Officer Second Class Matthew Bacile claims it was a favorite with guys in his group. They would squeeze the spread (reminiscent of any standard processed cheese spread) onto beef entrées for a cheeseburger-like effect.

"The jalapeño cheese was so bold that it covered up any bad flavor," Bacile says. "Some guys would mix everything together just to get it over with. If there was some kind of beef stew or something like that, they'd take everything and dump it all in together."

According to Air Force Staff Sergeant Jordan Jakubowski, with a few flameless ration heaters, you can make a small MRE firecracker to scare your friends. "Take the heater bag and put in a little water and then tie up two or three and shove them into a Gatorade bottle," Jakubowski says. "It'll swell up. Set it near someone, and it makes a loud pop."

He also explains that there's even a way to make an impromptu birthday cake. You take the powdered grape soda, add a little bit of water, and combine it with the milkshake powder. "Stir it up to where it's like a cake frosting and spread it on the cracker," he say. "We've done that for a few of the poor guys that had birthdays while out there." ⓛⓟ

SEAFARMING
at THE END *of*
THE WORLD

by PETER
MEEHAN

photographs by
GABRIELE
STABILE

Things are not looking good in our oceans and seas, our bays and waterways, our rivers and streams. Not for the things that live in them and, increasingly, not for the people who live along them.

The International Programme on the State of the Ocean, a group of oceanographers and other aquatically minded scientists, gathered at Oxford University in 2011 and published the findings of their symposium, which they summarized rather tidily: "The combination of stressors on the ocean is creating the conditions associated with every previous major extinction of species in Earth's history."

This scenario doesn't seem to dim Bren Smith's enthusiasm for raising imperiled sea creatures. Bren, who originally sent me the report, cheerily shouted to me, "WE'RE IN THE MIDDLE OF ONE OF THE LARGEST EXTINCTIONS IN THE OCEAN EVER!" as his oyster boat threaded its way through the Thimble Islands off the coast of Connecticut.

I visited him on the upper side of the Long Island Sound, where he works, a few weeks after flooding from a storm had muddied the waters—muddy waters suffocate oysters, not to mention his business—and it would be only a matter of weeks before Hurricane Sandy would come and deliver to him and his oysters another ruinous walloping. "I've been wiped out three times out of the last ten years—I mean completely wiped out," Bren says, "including last year, the entire crop."

Bren's operation is notable because its model is newish: a "3-D sea farm," he calls it. He raises mussels and scallops near the top of the water, and clams and oysters along the Sound's floor. Kelp, which grows during the winter, connects the two. The acreage his operation covers is minimal compared to its output—at least when the New Weather isn't busy killing what he raises.

I went out with him to slurp some oysters and talk about seafarming at the end of the world.

WHERE ARE WE?

We were in the Thimble Islands, a little-known East Coast archipelago of privately owned islands—some small enough for just one dwelling, several large enough to hold a host of houses.

All the homes are private. You know what's crazy? They've found some old Model Ts on one of the islands; back when the winters were colder, the water would freeze solid enough that you could commute to work over the ice. Now it's mostly summer places. Six of them are owned by this woman who's a magnate from a party store who got obsessed with collecting these islands and bought one for every one of her kids and grandkids. Rich people's business.

Some are rented—not quite time shares, exactly. Some of the older families, sort of the Connecticut Yankees who are land rich and cash poor, pay off their taxes by renting them out for a week. There's actually one sort-of advertised hotel out there, where you can rent the whole building, but it's mainly a really tight-knit community. The kids just keep coming back; even the working-class people here go back generations. It's that classic sort of island thing where sometimes you hate each other, but for the most part you love the place and the people and never want to leave.

There's a quarry on Bear Island where this famous pink granite comes from. The Statue of Liberty, the Brooklyn Bridge, Congress—they're all made out of the pink granite from that island and a quarry nearby on the mainland. And—this is a little in dispute but I know it for sure—when Howard Roark stands on the quarry's edge in Ayn Rand's *The Fountainhead*, that's on Bear Island over there.

HOW DID YOU GET HERE?

I grew up in Newfoundland in a little fishing village with nine houses. I dropped out of high school when I was fourteen and moved to Gloucester. Somebody told me I was a child laborer, but I was like, "All Newfies drop out of school." At fourteen, I even felt like I was a little late to do so! Then I

went to Alaska for about five years from when I was about sixteen. I went back and forth—I was on crab boats, cod boats, trawling, longlining, and so on. So the first half of my fishing career was like the worst form of food production. I was a complete raper and pillager up in Alaska. We didn't know better, or I didn't. I used to fish for McDonald's and they'd take all the sea lice–ridden, wormy fish—just the worst stuff.

I'm actually the worst oysterman ever, because I get seasick. Up in the Bering Sea, we'd be out for three months at a time. It's just brutal in the belly of the boat. I'd puke for the first two weeks, and after that I'd be fine. No one ever works through seasickness, you know? A lot of us used to get seasick the first two weeks.

I still work all the time. I haven't taken a vacation in six years, not even a weekend. And I love this— every second of it. Though I do eat terribly. I just don't have the time or money to do better. I'm an expert at putting together a gas-station dinner. We don't cook; my wife is an artist. When we moved here we lived in an old Airstream trailer for seven years while we built our house so we didn't have heat, a bathroom, or any way to cook. We'd just eat out every night. We didn't shop, and are still stuck in that rut.

WHAT IS SEAFARMING?

I got turned off by industrial fishing in part because the fish just started to disappear. I was starting to get some level of slow consciousness there, and I started to explore aquaculture. Of course, aquaculture was just beginning to get industrialized as land culture was getting deindustrialized, so my first exposure to it was terrible. I worked at some salmon farms, and they were awful. Very awful. I finally got interested in more of a self-directed life: owning my own life—not so much owning my own company but owning my own experiments and failures. I decided I wanted to take my life and be sustainable. I was sick of working for people, mainly. That's when I stumbled onto the idea of oystering.

Of course, oyster grounds are hard to get. The shellfishing grounds in this area are mainly owned by five families. But in 2005, the powers that be released grounds here for the first time in 150 years to attract people under forty back into fishery. A bunch of us tried and got in. I'm one of the last ones standing. Everyone else bought boats, went into debt, things like that. They were all fishermen, but this is not fishing—this is farming. Fishing is when you're chasing things, trying to hit the fish; fishing is like playing the lottery. But out here it's about touching every oyster and clam, every five weeks, keeping 'em free of anything unwanted, shaping them. (*Bren rubs off the brittle front edges of the oyster shells as they are growing, giving them a deeper, more cupped shape.*) It's really more like farming.

I've got sixty acres, but I do most of my production in just twenty of it. Beautiful thing is that I have this really small footprint. It's vertical farming. On top, on the longlines, I grow kelp and *Gracilaria*, a red seaweed. Below them, mussels are hanging in socks and scallops in lantern cages, and below that are oysters and clams. This is the first multispecies vertical ocean farm in the country. I'm the first one ever to get permitted for surface gear on Long Island Sound. It took me two years and an incredible amount of money to get the permits. The reason is the aesthetics. A lot of these very wealthy people don't want to see anything on the water even though they're foodies and environmentalists. Luckily here in the Thimbles I've gotten tremendous support from the local community.

These species that I raise here filter out carbon, nitrogen, even heavy metals. (Thank God we don't have that problem here in the Thimble Islands, but it is a reason to grow oysters in other places— not for eating, but to help clean up polluted waterways.) Besides what the shellfish do on their own, their cages function as artificial reefs—everything is attracted to 'em; we've counted 150 different species in these waters, way beyond what you'd normally expect to see these days.

We're getting a lot of creatures from down south. I just found a seahorse. No one's ever seen so many tropical fish around here. This year's been incredible. Four or five times already this summer, fishermen have been catching these crazy fish—tropical fish—that are coming because of the water-temperature changes.

The other reason no one's doing this 3-D seafarming thing is that it's so experimental: I'll run it at

a loss for quite a while because the kelp market already exists, it's mainly foreign, and there's a lot of local competition. We have to figure out how to Americanize it. I've got to get up to some economy of scale. Next year two more long lines will go in. I'll see how it goes as it grows. But I think you can only do local farming at my small scale and make a living by having some soft-subsidy model where I'm growing food for local communities, doing a lot of education work, working with kids, nonprofits, legislators, and scientists.

WHAT WAS AND WILL BE

There used to be oyster reefs so big here—like six feet high—that you'd actually have to navigate your boats around them. Oysters are a foundational species: they're the base of the ecosystem, which attracts everything, just like a coral reef. Take the Chesapeake Bay: the entire bay used to be filtered out once a week by the oysters. There were hundreds of millions of them! Oysters pull all the algae out of the water. When there's nothing to do that, you get huge algae blooms, which suck up all the oxygen and lead to higher nitrogen levels in the water. When the algae dies, it falls to the bottom and smothers what's down there, and you end up with these huge dead zones. Oysters were the natural buffer against that problem, but we killed them off so thoroughly that they can't come back on their own. Wild oysters are effectively gone.

Some scientists think oysters are going to be the first ocean species to be driven extinct by climate change. They're a very delicate crop and thrive at very particular temperatures. The acidification of the oceans weakens their shells. Disease spreads as the water temperatures rise. And when a hurricane storm surges and loosens up all the silt and dirt that's in our waterways now, the oysters drown in mud. Irene was the biggest storm surge since 1938. It was a big deal, and three feet of mud came in, which was bad. But the real bad news was that it loosened up the bottom here, so now smaller storms are bringing in more mud and having an outsize impact.

Oysters are used to filtering thirty to fifty gallons of water a day. If they're coated in mud, they just die. A clam can squish up and move. Same thing with scallops. Oysters are stuck wherever they are. That's why, with the BP spill in the Gulf, they did most of their testing on oysters. Oysters can't flee, regardless of how they feel about the water conditions.

There's a debate in the scientific community. I don't want to stand here and tell you oysters are gonna go away. There are hopeful people who believe in adaptation. The question is the speed. Oysters showed up something like 300 million years before dinosaurs. Before any fish. They've done well. The question is just how much and how fast they can change, and how they deal with the pressure we're putting on them. We're helping to extend their life through farming, but we're having incredible die-offs on the West Coast, where they're losing hundreds of millions of

oysters. They think it's because of the acidification that comes with rising temperatures.

So it's actually the twin evils of greenhouse gases: climate change and ocean acidification. They're very linked because the ocean soaks up a third of the carbon in the world and we've maxed it out as a carbon sink. It pulls out way more carbon than land-based plants like tropical forests. And all of that leads to water temperatures rising and a changed pH that affects the shells of mollusks and crustaceans. They're finding all these other odd things as well, like that fish are getting much smaller, not just because of overfishing but because of the changing temperatures. I just read this thing where they got forty of the top oceanographers in the world and they said we're in the middle of one of the largest extinctions in the ocean ever. Like, the top three or something, and we're not at the beginning of it: we're in the middle of it. This is happening. So the news is bad.

So you can stop overfishing, you can create huge marine parks, and everything's gonna die anyway. My argument is that it's not about conservation anymore, it's about development. It's not "How do we save the oceans?" but "How do the oceans save us?" Let's move beyond depletion—even beyond restoration—to a place where we're actually improving the environment and fixing all these other social problems, from jobs to climate change. This is where I always get in fights with conservationists and environmentalists. I think we need an industrial policy to create local food, create fuel, pull nitrogen and carbon

out of the system, and to do it by creating good jobs on the water. I mean, I am a deeply self-interested party who may be prone to exaggeration and lying, but I think kelp farming and this sort of integrated aquaculture we're doing here really could be an answer.

I mean, the kelp alone! My seaweed pulls five times the amount of carbon as a tree out of the water. Because kelp grows so fucking fast and it doesn't take much area. My first mate, Ron, and I can create thousands and thousands and thousands of pounds of seaweed. And you could dot the coastline with these kinds of farms. With agriculture, what do we normally compete for? Land and fresh water. I don't use any of that.

I'm addicted to kelp. It's an ocean farmer's dream: fastest growing plant in the world, and it's a winter crop, which is invaluable for me. I'll plant next month, by March we'll have six to twelve feet—just stunning. It's our East Coast native sugar kelp and it can be used in cooking just like Japanese kombu. There are some slight differences between the two, but not in terms of taste. And like kombu it's high in iron, calcium, potassium, and magnesium; it's got B vitamins and vitamin C, and iodine and zinc. It's also a really rich source of iron. There are all these other uses, too. I'm working with a biofuel company here in Connecticut. You take a one-acre area and you get 2,000 gallons of ethanol per year.

The process for turning kelp into fuel is much faster than it is for land-based fuel—two or three times as fast to process kelp. They basically just liquefy it. We could use the high-quality stuff grown in clean water for food, fertilizer, and fish food, and I could grow kelp in very polluted areas—places where the water is chock full of heavy metals—and use it for biofuel and other things, too.

And we can scale up. I can't even believe the numbers coming out of the scientific literature—you take 3 percent of the oceans and dedicate them to seaweed and you can actually fuel the world. With an area half the size of Maine you can replace all the oil in the United States.

There's a counterargument to what I'm talking about that says this is about financializing or exploiting the environment in the name of saving it. There's some truth to that, but I think we're past the point where we can pretend like sitting around and not touching anything will save us. Things are too far gone. I'm not some industrialist. I am deeply, deeply of this new generation of green fishermen, protecting the environment both for life and livelihood. God, I sound mad, don't I? "Forty acres and a mule! Life and livelihood!"

But this isn't about altruism. It's actually about feeding and paying people—making this truly sustainable. Food activists have to start thinking about this: how to make a living, how to have pensions, how to move subsidies off the industrial farms and over to the small ones, how to make farming a real job. We need a working class of equal dignified professionals—not just poor farmers or workers.

If you're actually modeling this out and can get a lot of people to do it, it will create jobs and food, and it will be good for the water. It drives me nuts when I hear about people who want to go back to agrarian culture. They haven't thought it through. We can't walk away from this coast and come back in twenty years and expect it to be covered in oysters. That's not going to happen. As an oysterman, how can I address climate change? I can't go to Kentucky to stop coal plants. I can grow kelp. That's how I can help.

Regardless of what happens, it's a wonderful time to be alive. History's moving so fast and we're doomed and I'm Irish and the great thing about life is that it's short. This is how I want my hours spent, out here, doing this as long as I can. It's hard work. It's not profitable and it destroys your body. I crawl out of bed like a crab every morning. My back's gone, my shoulders are going, and most of the time my hands are so rough my wife makes me have sex like a lobster.

I hope we can turn the tide back a bit—create more jobs and better food along our coasts—but hope isn't my thing. Work is. And I'll keep working these waters until the storms and the banks shut me down. What I usually say is this: just as I remade myself a green fisherman, I'm going to be part of the first generation of green fishermen put out of work.

But I think the answer with oysters and shellfish is an adaptation strategy. Can we work hard now so another generation of fishermen, with new techniques and technologies, can earn a living out here? Long term, it doesn't look good. But you never know. ⓛⓟ

POLLUTION

Cuttlefish, calamari, clams, sea urchin, monkfish liver | *Makes 4 servings*

Dehydrate lettuces → Make sea broth → Emulsify liver cream → Make lemon froth → Marinate seafood; serve

In many places—the atolls of the Pacific, the shrimp beds of the Eastern Seaboard, the fjords of Norway—some of the most advanced forms of ocean life are struggling to survive while the most primitive are thriving and spreading. Fish, corals and marine mammals are dying while algae, bacteria, and jellyfish are growing unchecked. Where this pattern is most pronounced, scientists evoke a scenario of evolution running in reverse, returning to the primeval seas of hundreds of millions of years ago.

—*Kenneth Weiss*, Altered Oceans

As coastlines froth with oil, algae, and toxic nitrogen, primitive organisms are returning from the distant past. Naturally the metamorphosis of pelagic life will define what we eat.

"Pollution" is a chilly prediction of a future swimming in Cimmerian smudge, what I imagine Cormac McCarthy means when he says: "The ponderous counterspectacle of things ceasing to be." It is a dish I conceived at the first Cook It Raw, held in Copenhagen in 2009, an event in which chefs from around the world gather together to cook with what's available in the environment around them. When I look to the natural world, I cannot help but see the dangers inherent in only seeing nature as a source of ingredients.

The dish is visually modeled after a polluted beach, an approximation of what may lie ahead: filth-smattered coasts, littered with the remains of sea life. Flavor-wise, it is a bit less macabre.

—**MASSIMO BOTTURA, OSTERIA FRANCESCANA**

INGREDIENTS & EQUIPMENT

+	sea lettuces (dulce, carrageenan, wakame, etc.)
50 g	cuttlefish, cleaned and sliced thin
12	baby calamari, tentacles only
12	shucked Veraci clams
4	sea urchin tongues
+	sea fennel, glasswort, Szechuan buttons, tarragon, and blanched seaweed for garnish
+	dehydrator
+	Thermomix (opt.)
+	vacuum sealer and immersion circulator (opt.)

SEA BROTH

50 g	glasswort
3	oysters
a few drops	squid ink
+	salt

LIVER CREAM

40 g	monkfish liver
30 g	foie gras
7 g	salt
9 g	white sugar
8 g	sake
4 g	soy sauce

LEMON FROTH

100 g	lemon juice
50 g	water
40 g	sugar
a pinch	soy lecithin

SEAFOOD MARINADE

30 g	lemon juice
a pinch	lemon zest
50 g	clam juice
2 g	chopped celery
2 g	chopped shallots
a pinch	fresh chopped chili

1 **Wash sea lettuces very thoroughly** in mineral water. Dry in a dehydrator at 40°C for 2 days, then pulverize in a spice grinder.

2 **Glasswort is a salty coastal plant**, also known as sea bean. There's not really a substitute for it, but if you know what to look for, it's quite common and easy to find in the wild.

Blanch the glasswort in boiling water for a minute, then plunge into ice cold water. Blend with cold water—3 parts glasswort to 2 parts water—until smooth.

3 **Add the oysters, oyster liquid, and squid ink** to the puréed glasswort, and blend until smooth. Season with a touch of salt. Pass the purée through a sieve, then chill.

4 **Clean the monkfish liver and foie gras of all veins**. Cut into small pieces and let marinate sous vide with the other liver-cream ingredients for 24 hours. If you don't have a vacuum sealer, place the livers in a Ziploc bag and press/suck out as much air as possible.

5 **Cook the livers at 55°C**, vacuum sealed, in an immersion circulator for 30 minutes. Without an immersion circulator, place the bag of livers under a very hot faucet for 30 minutes.

Remove the livers and blend until smooth. Strain through a sieve.

6 **Place the livers in a bowl** over another bowl filled with ice. Whisk the cooked livers into a creamy emulsion and place into a piping bag. Chill.

7 **Blend together all the lemon froth ingredients** except the soy lecithin in a Thermomix set at 50°C for 5 minutes. (A normal blender will work if you don't have a Thermomix.) Chill until ready to serve. Just before serving, add the soy lecithin and whip the mixture with an immersion blender until a foam forms.

8 **Blend all the seafood marinade ingredients** together and strain through a fine-mesh strainer. Chill for at least 6 hours.

9 **20 minutes before serving**, marinate the seafood—each specimen in its own plastic bag with an equitable share of marinade. Strain the marinade before serving.

10 **Gather all the dish components and garnishes.** Place the cuttlefish, tentacles, clams, and sea urchin at the bottom of a shallow bowl. Top with Szechuan buttons and four small mounds of liver cream. Sprinkle sea-lettuce powder on top. Cover everything ¾ of the way with broth, and surround with seaweed. Finish with herbs and lemon froth.

Dish photo by Per-Anders Jorgensen

SHELF LIFE

FERMENTING INTO THE FUTURE WITH SANDOR KATZ

ILLUSTRATIONS BY PAUL WINDLE

The idea that anyone could accurately know when the apocalypse will arrive or how it will look is absurd. Yet many of us imagine various doomsday scenarios, most of which are quite plausible and perhaps even likely: environmental collapse due to pollution and resource extraction; increasingly volatile weather wreaking devastation; nuclear war; new diseases; genetic manipulation gone haywire; artificial intelligence gone awry; UFOs; the wrath of God... it is not unreasonable to feel like the shit may indeed soon hit the fan.

Collapse is already happening. We can see it in accelerating extinctions, as well as in resource depletion, rising tides and worsening storms, floods and droughts and crop failures, and emerging diseases. Whenever and however things change, we will fare much better—and eat better fare—if we empower ourselves with some basic survival skills now.

Among those skills is the thoroughly useful and rewarding practice of preservation through fermentation. For millennia, humans have harnessed the powers of microorganisms to turn fresh food into more shelf-stable (as well as more digestible and delicious) products.

Bacteria and fungi offer metabolic pathways into the future that can help us survive. These microorganisms have been found to decompose many pollutants including petroleum and many of its by-products, the phthalates used in plastics and cosmetics, and the organophosphorus compounds used in pesticides, plasticizers, jet fuel, and chemical weapons. Bacteria have the capability to incorporate new genes and shed unneeded ones, giving them unparalleled shape-shifting mutability. If our evolutionary imperative is to adapt to shifting conditions, then we must embrace, encourage, and work with microorganisms.

VESSELS

The first essential items are vessels. For most ferments, I use ceramic crocks, wooden barrels, glass jars, jugs, and carboys. Purchase, reuse, scavenge, or learn to make any of these. Gourds are thought to have been the earliest of cultivated plants, selected for their usefulness as vessels for fermented beverages (as well as water). The most ancient vessel is probably a pit in the ground lined with layers of leaves, grasses, and other botanical barriers. Increasingly, I'm using hand-crafted crocks (the ceramic arts were originally inspired by the need for fermentation vessels) in many different shapes, some quite beautiful.

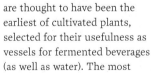
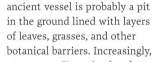
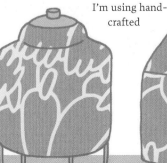

SALT

Salt is an important element of many different ferments. It was among the earliest of commodities, traded across vast distances. Although it is not present in concentrated form in many locations, it is necessary to supplement the limited essential sodium naturally occurring in our food, and facilitates much food preservation. Stockpile now or start evaporating seawater!

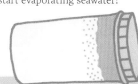

STARTERS

There are many types of starters, including pure-strain yeasts, bacteria, molds, broader microbial communities such as yogurt and sourdough, and symbiotic communities of bacteria and yeast (SCOBYs), which are embodied in a physical form, such as kombucha and kefir. Most of these starter cultures require periodic feeding and attention in order to survive. It is possible to store them for long periods of time by drying and/or refrigerating and/or freezing. (Since refrigeration options may be limited in the hellscape of the future, caves, cellars, and other perpetually cool-to-cold hiding places may be your next best bet.)

If you are already maintaining one or more specific starter cultures and they should survive the apocalypse with you, make sure to share them. The easiest form of perpetuation is backslopping: introducing a small amount of one batch to start the next. The fermenting vessel or a stirring device (dedicated to this purpose and unwashed) can also serve as a means of perpetuation. If your supply dies, someone whom you shared it with may be able to backslop you back into business.

Without any preexisting starters, there is always wild fermentation, initiated by organisms naturally present on food or in the environment. Until a century ago, almost all traditional ferments were made by means of wild fermentation, and generally the best still are. Fruits are covered in yeast, vegetables with lactic acid bacteria, and beans and grains with both.

SUBSTRATES

Substrates are the nutrients upon which you are growing communities of microorganisms or, more plainly, the food you are fermenting! Substrates are the substance of fermentation, the stuff that's being transformed: vegetables; grapes and other fruits; milk; meat and fish; honey and sugar; wheat, barley, soy, and other grains and beans. The real challenge of post-apocalypse fermentation will be obtaining food to ferment.

The procurement of food is a fundamental activity for survival for all beings. We have created elaborate systems of production and distribution to distance ourselves from this essential biological reality, but in any apocalypse scenario survivors will most assuredly be reminded of it. Do not wait for necessity to force you to start acquiring the skills to produce and/or forage at least some food yourself! Growing plants, raising animals, and recognizing wild edibles are all cyclical activities with long learning curves.

The time to start on that path is now! Becoming a food producer and getting involved in a network of like-minded others means sharing and exchanging homegrown food and rebuilding local economies with greater resilience, so that whatever happens, we have some skills and some small measure of food security. **LP**

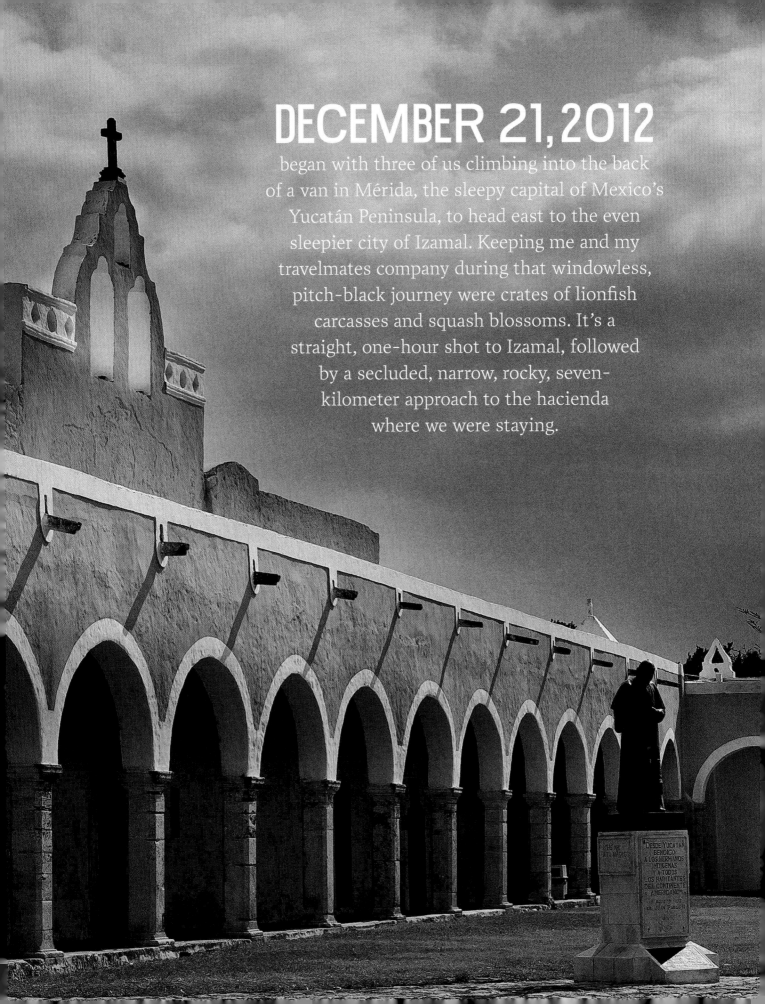

DECEMBER 21, 2012

began with three of us climbing into the back of a van in Mérida, the sleepy capital of Mexico's Yucatán Peninsula, to head east to the even sleepier city of Izamal. Keeping me and my travelmates company during that windowless, pitch-black journey were crates of lionfish carcasses and squash blossoms. It's a straight, one-hour shot to Izamal, followed by a secluded, narrow, rocky, seven-kilometer approach to the hacienda where we were staying.

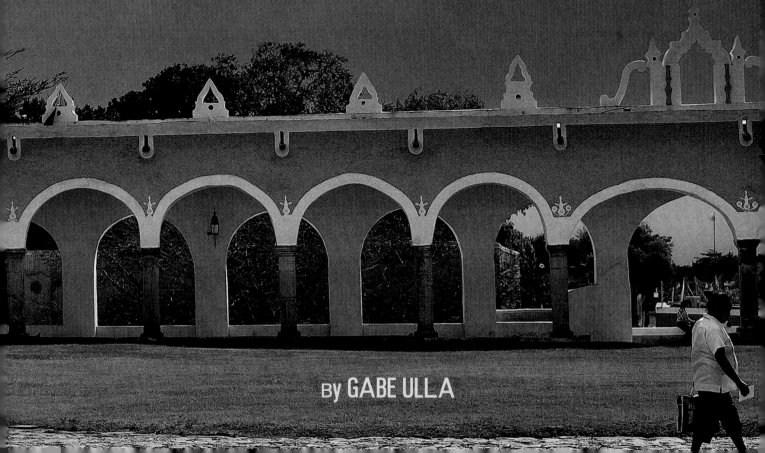

DINNER WITH THE MAYANS

IN WHICH MEXICO'S BEST CHEFS—AND ONE DANISH FRIEND—COOK DINNER ON THE LAST NIGHT ON EARTH.

BY GABE ULLA

There, spread throughout the property's outdoor kitchen, were some of Mexico's most notable chefs: Enrique Olvera, Alejandro Ruiz, Guillermo González Beristain, Benito Molina, and local representative Roberto Solís. Also present: token Danish emissary René Redzepi. It was around five. The lionfish went to Molina, and the squash blossoms to Olvera. Some of the chefs put the finishing touches on their *mises en place*, while others told stories and fucked around. All had Coronitas by their side.

Chef Jair Téllez emerged from the wilderness tenuously hoisting a substantial silver pot he had just pulled from the earth. Téllez, who runs restaurants in Baja California and Mexico City, had chosen to prepare a *pib*, essentially an underground oven, using a technique that dates back to Mayan times. Making a pib requires digging a deep hole in the dirt, setting leaves and hot stones at the bottom, and placing the covered pot in the cavity. The items within cook at a low temperature, and for a long time. In this particular case, Téllez prepared an array of local vegetables: chayas, yuca, camotes, carrots, and other items he'd conjured from the vicinity—evidence that confirmed we were in the middle of the jungle. Téllez placed the pot on the counter. All of the other chefs, on their tiptoes, took turns peering in and having a sniff.

A few hours and several beers later, it was time to pack up Tellez's vegetables to head into the center of town. The world was about to end, and we weren't about to let that happen without a celebration.

The Dinner of the New Baktun would take place that evening, outdoors in the convent of San Antonio de Padua, which boasts one of the largest atriums in the world. The *baktun* is an increment of time equivalent to 144,000 days, or, if you want to be Mayan about it, twenty *katun* cycles of the Long Count Calendar. December 21, 2012 marked the end of the thirteenth baktun, the last one outlined in the Mayan calendar. Some around the world interpreted this finality as a signal of the end of it all, for everybody. The events' organizers saw it as the ideal moment to get together some of the country's great chefs—and their noted Danish friend—for dinner in an epic setting. The chefs saw the evening as a chance to cook with friends and get their ya-yas out.

By 8 p.m., most fears of the end—if there had been any legitimate ones at all—had faded. The chefs convened with their teams, fresh beers in hand. Some of them, observing that they were working an open kitchen in full view of ninety or so diners (most of them Mexican journalists and enthusiasts who could afford a $400 meal) decided to conceal their booze consumption, emptying their water bottles and filling them with mezcal.

In the right-back corner of the kitchen, Redzepi stood alone harboring less apocalyptic fears. "It's supposed to start at ten, but I don't think that's going to happen," he offered to me as I approached his station. "Some people are saying it might actually be closer to eleven thirty, but I don't know." Back home at his restaurant Noma, Redzepi is

used to rising early, working late, and commanding an army of cooks and stagiaires. Here, in a temporary kitchen in the middle of a Yucatecan field, Redzepi was struggling to figure out how to get coals burning and how to time his dish—the first of the evening.

Redzepi hadn't flown in Scandinavian juniper or moss or wood sorrel for the occasion. Instead, he chose to envision what it might have been like to eat in Mayan times, devising a salad of mango, yuca, Yucatecan pumpkin, pineapple coated on one side with a layer of spicy, funky *recado negro*, watermelon, star fruit, avocado, and herbs. Many of the components were marinated and grilled, and the dish was anchored by a broth of grilled-tomato water, *epazote*, mint, cilantro, chili oil, and fermented cep (porcini) juice. "These are things I can't use in Copenhagen," said Redzepi of his ingredient choices. Still, there was something fundamentally Noma about his effort, beyond just the aesthetics of his plate. As he does at home in Denmark, he was preparing what made sense there and at that moment.

Yet Redzepi's face suggested that his current place and time were beginning to provoke a few frustrations. He was, as one perceptive local cook pointed out, in danger of becoming familiar with *el desmadre*. Literally, the motherless situation. Loosely, the moment when people have let loose, or worse, the shit has hit the fan. It was 9 p.m. and there hadn't yet been a meeting between the chefs about service. (I'm not sure there ended up ever being one.) Molina's lionfish would not be

Photos by Alberto Cáceres

served *en crudo*, as the printed menu suggested. No one was quite sure when guests would arrive or exactly how many there would be. Yet the fact remained that these guys were meant to stage a meal so remarkable that a diner would be content calling it his or her last.

At 9:45, guests began to arrive. Noticing that the talent was out in the open, they swarmed the kitchen and began to chat up the chefs. The chefs, most having long ago resigned themselves to the social obligations of their positions, obliged.

About twenty minutes later, the diners trickled back to the field and into their chairs. A first snack course left the kitchen. Redzepi began plating his dish in the ninety bowls he had purchased earlier in the day at the town market. He quickly beckoned for the attention of his colleagues, who were still lined up in front of the kitchen

taking questions from diners, and asked for their help. Suddenly everyone—chefs, cooks, waiters, volunteers, stagiaires—surrounded Redzepi in a flurry of activity. Redzepi poured tomato broth into the first bowl, the finishing touch, and Olvera briskly took it out of the kitchen. Dinner had begun.

And so it went for the next two hours and seven courses, with only a few negligible hiccups.

At one point during the evening, the archaeologist Alice Gamboa verbalized a less alarmist reading of the Mayan calendar: "Today we are celebrating a new beginning, a time to wash away the ills of the past and move forward into a new era." A careful observer of restaurant cooking in Mexico would have noted that the chefs on hand had gotten a head start on that process

some time ago.

"I don't think this would have been possible five years ago," said the bespectacled, imposingly tall Beristain as he surveyed that night's kitchen, packed to the brim with cooks from all over the country. What has happened in Mexico's kitchens over the last decade is remarkable. A number of chefs—several of whom were present—have embraced Mexico's traditional foodways and developed restaurants that are now considered among the best in the world.

One factor that made this pronounced evolution possible is the fact that the chefs went outside before coming back in. Olvera and Beristain first studied at the Culinary Institute of America. Téllez went to the French Culinary Institute, and Molina received his formal culinary training at the New England Culinary Institute in Vermont. Téllez tells

tales of peeling potatoes for Alex Lee at Daniel; Roberto Solís had a life-changing experience spending time at the Fat Duck; and Olvera got a visa so that he could spend six months working around Chicago.

Yet exposure to great kitchens in America and Europe didn't inspire these chefs to open French or Italian restaurants in Mexico. Olvera explained to me that he and his colleagues came back with a sense of freedom, able to honor their traditions while occasionally reexamining them. Olvera has emerged as the leading representative of the new Mexican cuisine. He is the chef and owner of Pujol in Mexico City and organizer of the ambitious annual Mesamérica Festival, which brings the country's chefs—both progressive and more traditional—together with major players from abroad to promote Mexican cuisine and exchange ideas.

The result of these efforts has been a shift away from the Eurocentrism of Mexican diners. It used to be that the great restaurants in Mexico City weren't cooking Mexican. Now, if you want a good meal, you head to Jorge Vallejo's Quintonil, or Pujol, or Gabriela Cámara's Contramar—all of which are cooking decidedly Mexican food (albeit in some cases unconventionally so). Most important, perhaps, is how the work of these chefs has further advanced the idea that "Mexican" is a highly regionalized cuisine. It includes everything from the traditional to Olvera's progressive takes on his city's street food, from Alejandro Ruiz's command of Oaxaca's notoriously vast canon, to Téllez and Molina's ability to draw from

the landscape and waters of Baja to develop a cuisine that might have more in common with the Mediterranean than with Mexico City.

Ricardo Muñoz Zurita is the chef of the Azul restaurants in Mexico City and the author of eleven books. His most recent, the *Larousse Dictionary of Mexican Gastronomy*, provides detailed definitions of Mexican ingredients and techniques, including how preparations differ from region to region. He attended the end-of-the-world dinner and stayed at the hacienda. As both an academic authority and member of the community of chefs, he boils down the advancement of Mexican cuisine to preparation and mastery of technique. "I hate to say it, but it used to be that chefs in Mexico didn't learn their craft as well as these newer generations have," Zurita says. "These chefs are highly cultured, many of them speak more than one language, and because of all of this, there's a richness to the gastronomic scene that is unprecedented."

Zurita points out one other crucial factor: a spirit of fraternity that rivals that of any restaurant scene in the world. That night's dinner was a good example. Working quietly in the kitchen were notable chefs who hadn't been invited as headliners. Among these volunteers were Alfredo Villanueva and Paulino Cruz, who had made the trips from Monterrey and Mexico City, respectively, just to help out their friends.

"Yes, we're happy that Mexico's culinary scene is being recognized, and we want to push that forward," says Olvera. "At the same time, though, the desire to come together and do that might be driven less by

nationalism and more by the simple fact that we love each other."

The sense of fraternity became clearest to me after the paying diners had left, the lights were shut off in the convent, and only the chefs were left to horse around and drink *calimochos*—a sublime mix of red wine and Coca-Cola. Redzepi had already retired to the hacienda. Olvera and Beristain laughed like hyenas as a cook from Argentina took out his phone and started up an app that played the *Indiana Jones* theme and made the sounds of a whiplash on command.

On the drive back, Juan Luis Guerra and LCD Soundsystem sloppily blasted from the weak sound system. We paused once to step out of the car and marvel at the supernaturally black and starry sky above us. "We saw a jaguar on this road last night, by the way," muttered Villanueva.

Back at the hacienda, they parked the car in front of the main building and set it up as a makeshift DJ booth. Throughout the evening, bottles of mezcal and beer accumulated on the hood of the car, and everybody danced. At one point, the Argentinean surfaced from the kitchen with chicken and venison sandwiches. The party didn't die down until six in the morning.

Over the next two days, the hacienda emptied. Some, like Téllez, had restaurants to check up on, while others sped home for Christmas. Everyone left with other things to attend to, but hoping that the world might end just a bit more often. 🅛🅟

SEEKING SHELTER

The apocalypse will have nothing to do with fire raining from the sky or the undead knocking at your door. Its root is Greek—*apokalyptein*, feminine, concerning truths once unknown, now visible to all. The darkness brought into light. Armageddon may not come in our lifetime, but the grid may fail or we may render our cities uninhabitable. We may face the unknown.

This is exactly why Lloyd Kahn was put on this earth. Lloyd started building houses in the '60s and publishing countercultural texts in the '70s. As a child, I pored over the picture-dense pages of *Shelter*, Lloyd's book of unconventional habitats, imagining ways to live that didn't involve the stucco houses on TV. Lloyd's books still give me the strange comfort of knowing that I can always turn to them if I ever need a blueprint for the kind of largely forgotten skills and wisdom that it will take to get by in a handbuilt and hand-to-mouth world. These photos, which he was gracious enough to share, come from his archives. —CHRISTINE BOEPPLE

There are more than 12,000 kinds of mosses, overly abundant in areas of dampness and shade. Mosses absorb moisture, have a high drought tolerance and are incredibly light weight—making them an ideal roofing material, insulator, diaper, or bed.

A saw and a hammer will be your new computer and smart phone.

Seawater-soaked driftwood has a high chlorine content, so it's better to build with it than to burn it. Think about the beach property you could have in the summertime.

The difference between squab and pigeon? *Lifestyle.*

Scavenging will be your full-time job.

Squirrels taste better.

With a little education you can turn roadkill into an awesome pelt to cushion that driftwood chair you made.

What? You're a vegetarian? Haha. OK.

Bones are of endless interest. Left: bobcat bones found buried in a glade.

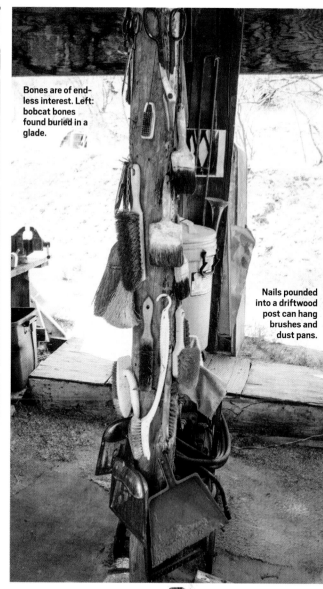

Nails pounded into a driftwood post can hang brushes and dust pans.

Build yourself a better view.

Fashion a carrier for firewood with some leather and rubber handles.

Two layers of concrete blocks on top of quarter-inch mesh, makes gopher-proof raised beds.

Self-sufficiency is a direction. You never really get there.

Use applewood, driftwood, pearwood, or plumwood to make a dragon handle for a copper pot.

You can't do *everything* for yourself. But you can figure out how much you *can* do.

The kitchen is the heart of every homestead.

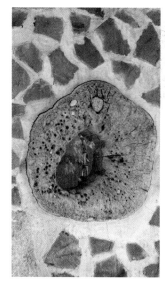

Do you know the difference between a pantry, scullery, larder, and kitchen?

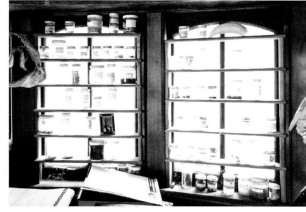

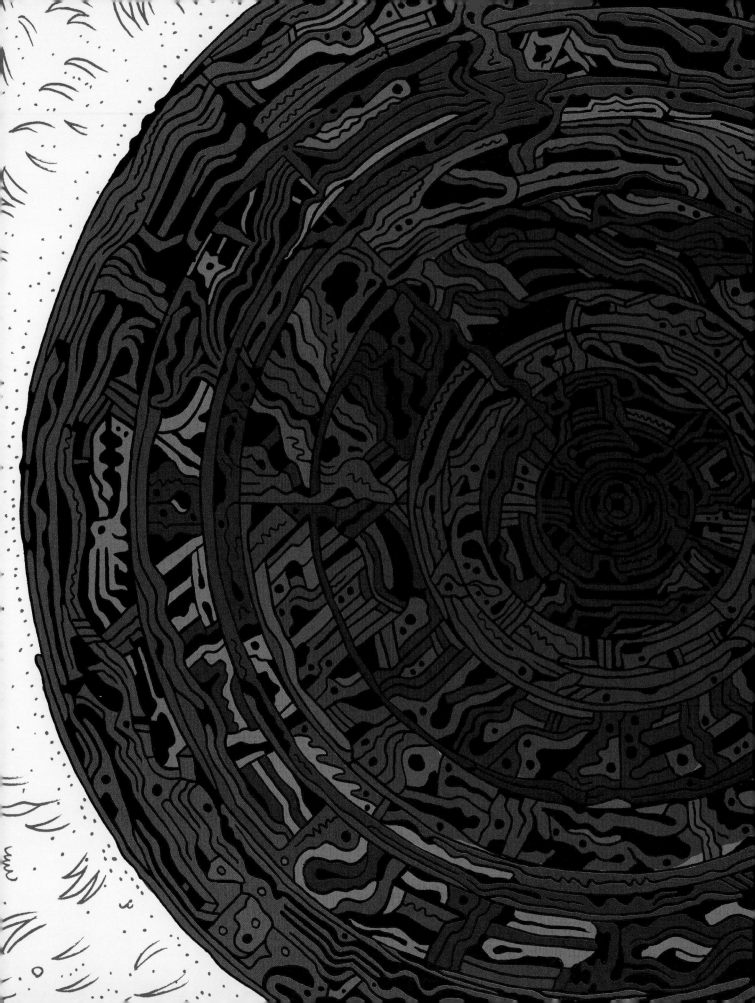

A STORY BY **BILL COTTER**

THE TRAPDOOR

ILLUSTRATED BY **RON REGÉ JR.**

Maryellen John lay along the backseat of her parents' chuggy, decrepit 2000 Nissan Altima, stiff with boredom, trying to unlock the rear driver's-side door with her toe. If she succeeded, she just might open it and let herself be sucked out onto the highway and get crushed by a cement truck or something. That would serve her mother right for taking back her iPad just as Maryellen was getting the hang of Drop it in the Hole, a habit-forming game based on the Hole, a geological novelty in Texas to which she and her parents were presently traveling.

Maryellen wondered what it would be like to fall in the Hole. Maryellen wondered what the Hole *was*, which was the same thing everyone else on the planet was wondering. How deep was it? What was at the bottom? Would more Holes open up elsewhere in the world? What if a Hole opened in the sea? Would all the water in the world drain away, leaving trillions of gasping fishes flopping around in vast, open valleys of yuck? And what if her parents fell in—would Maryellen feel sad? Yes, but less sad for her mother.

Maryellen still didn't understand what had happened between her parents; all she knew was that everything had been fine and then nothing was. The house became a clenched mouth of straining fury. She thought it might have something to do with money and other people. In any case, Maryellen was on her father's side. Maryellen always voted for the underdog, and her father seemed to be trailing quite a bit in whatever this rageous contest was that her parents were engaged in.

After a good half-hour's effort, Maryellen gave up trying to unlock the door. She began to kick it instead.

Ingrid John, her mother, who had reclaimed the iPad in order to work on that day's *New York Times* sudoku puzzle, Difficult, looked over her shoulder just long enough to say, "Stop that, please."

"No!" shouted Maryellen, kicking more rapidly, the soles of her Mary Janes producing a *depdepdepdep* that made Ingrid's sinuses ache. How Ingrid envied her little girl. How Ingrid would like to recline her seat, scream, and kick out the windshield. That's how she felt about the stupid concession stand. According to *bighole.com*, 150 vendors, mostly selling food, had already gathered there, surrounding the almost perfectly round 310-yard-wide geological void like kittens at a food dish. And now the John family were to be number 151. The last space. There would be no more.

They'd be there in a few hours. It would take them a day or so to set up their food truck, which David, Ingrid's husband, had named Hole Holes. David had mortgaged their house, bought a second-hand roach coach, decorated it from top to bottom with Hindu deities, outfitted it with a vast deep-fat fryer, a big Hobart mixer, and a genuine clay tandoor purchased at the liquidation sale of a floundered Indian restaurant; and dragged everything, including his family and a camper, off to live at the edge of a plumbless hole that had spontaneously opened up in the middle of the million-acre Kirkless Ranch in West Texas, swallowing a cashiered pumpjack, a section of barbed-wire fencing, and a cowboy named Ernesto.

Solution Incorrect, said the *New York Times* sudoku puzzle, Difficult.

"Damn it," said Ingrid.

"Dollar!" shouted Maryellen.

"Wrong again?" said David, gripping the steering wheel and squinting at the straight, endless West Texas highway.

Ingrid loosed a puffy, staccato sigh that signaled she had indeed lost. Losing at sudoku made her feel minimal and stupid. Ingrid wondered if Megan played sudoku. Megan, a chef David had once worked for, years before his marriage to Ingrid, had been entirely unknown to Ingrid until one night when David suddenly leapt out of a dead sleep to a standing position on the bed, and, through his habit of talkative somnambulism, pronounced his unrequited lust for this Megan, whom he went on to describe as a wine-haired bombshell who always had her fingers in her mouth, tasting sauces. After that, Megan, this historical figment, strode continually through the Johns' marriage, inciting arguments and silences and ugly midnight departures.

Later, Ingrid befriended Link, the chef at Suttling House, the Johns' Evanston, Illinois restaurant. Link grew to become the only person Ingrid had to talk to about Megan, this clot in her marriage. One night after closing, talking turned into fucking.

"So why play?" said David. "At least try Medium. Or Easy."

"I don't know. I just—"

"I know, I know, don't say it."

"I just don't understand why this whole thing is so attractive to you, David."

David began to giggle like a ninth-grader full of pot.

"That was punny!"

"Dam—"

"Dollar!" shouted Maryellen. "Another dollar for me!"

"I didn't say *it*, though, Maryellen, *did* I, so no dollar," said Ingrid.

"Two dollars!"

"Maryellen, please shut up," said David.

"She's going to fall in, I know," said Ingrid.

"No she won't. There's a fence. You can't get by without a pass and a guard. You saw the website."

"People get through all the time. And leap to their deaths."

This was true. The Hole had attracted many suicides in its six-month existence.

"Don't worry. She won't fall in. Will you, Maryellen?"

"Not if you give me the iPad back."

Ingrid handed it over.

"It'll be fine, Ingrid. We'll make a big pile of money, then sell the lease."

"You know what I think?" said Ingrid, going through the glove compartment, where she was sure she had stashed her copy of *Utterly Undoable Sudoku #41.* "I think you have a problem with women."

"What?"

"The Hole." Ingrid glanced over at her daughter, who was busy playing SodaMonger on the iPad, then whispered: "Men want to go see it and put things in it. They want to own it and control it. I think you want some fresh hole, David."

"Fresh? *I* want fresh? Look who's talking!"

David had caught Ingrid and Link screwing on the floor of Suttling House's coatroom one night after hours. Upon this discovery, David, in a gesture of jealous despair, had tried to eat the live fugu in the tank by the restaurant's entrance. But he was unable to catch the cunning animal, and was eventually chaperoned by policemen to Farritz, a private Evanston psychiatric facility. After a few weeks, David, on a cocktail of Sardonkin, Contentidol, Phalitax, and Bistec, was discharged to his impenitent wife and hysterical daughter. The release of Ingrid's jittery and delicate husband brought fresh resentments: Ingrid because she felt she'd cant her husband's mental balance if she got too mad at him; David because he knew this and hated being thought too fragile to engage. Meanwhile, the names Link and Megan rolled silently though the house, David and Ingrid carefully hopping over them when they approached, and blowing them off course when they threatened to collide.

The Hole fascinated everyone. People traveled to the ranch, forty miles from the nearest human settlement, to peer into the black of the Hole. Vendors at the Hole did well, especially the roach coaches. Many, many people came to see the Hole, and they brought cameras and money and appetites.

The Kirkless Ranch was officially in charge of the Hole, as it was on (in) private property, where the owners enjoyed full mineral estate. The Kirklesses controlled everything, including the number and nature of vendors. They had auctioned off most spots, some going for as much as a hundred thousand dollars. A few spots were awarded by lottery. This was how David and Ingrid John got theirs.

Suttling House had not been doing well. David had never done well with anything, but especially not with restaurants. But he persevered. When he was twenty-two, five years before he met Ingrid, David had gotten knocked prone by the bosom, cheekbones, and culinary skills of a chef named Megan Persoiles, who'd hired him as sous-chef for her restaurant, Massialot, and had just as quickly fired him for making a pass at her. Ever since, David had tried to become as successful a restaurateur as Megan was so that she would fall in love with him. But David was not that good. His restaurants tanked, one after another. Most people endure one business failure, perhaps two, and then return to retail or accounting or fraud or what have you. But David, for all his shortcomings, was good at finding investors, and so had been able to commit five sensational business failures in a row. By the time he opened Suttling House, he had pretty much reaped every potential investor in Evanston. Suttling House was his last chance.

Then the Hole opened up.

When the Johns received the letter confirming their lottery win, Ingrid suggested they sell their spot. They were sitting at the kitchen table when the letter came. David was fresh out of Farritz and the Hole was still big news. If they were lucky, Ingrid thought, they could walk away with a small fortune. Small fortunes could fix a lot of things, possibly even ailing marriages.

"I'll bet you can sell it for a couple hundred grand," she said, throwing fistfuls of hundred-dollar bills around in her head.

"*Sell* it?" David said. "No way we're *selling* it. We're *going* there. To get rich and famous."

Ingrid stared at David. A giant vacuum nozzle entered her head and sucked up all the hundreds.

"What are you going to *vend*?" said Ingrid, her tiny riser of hope that all might be well after all now crushed.

"Doughnut holes!"

"Funny."

"Serious."

"Right."

"Yep."

"Doughnut holes. C'mon."

"For people to eat, or throw in the Hole, you know, for luck."

"You're nuts."

"Plus chicken tikka masala," said David.

The sudden appearance of the Hole dislocated virtually every form of rational inquiry, from geology to philosophy to cosmogony to eschatology to economy to garbology to ufology. The ones most worked up were the geologists, who screamed theories at one another and mashed their foreheads into stone walls. The ones least in crisis were those scholars of the department of eschatology dealing with hell. The Hellists simply nodded to each other in grave certainty (and not without a bit of self-congratulation) that the end of the world was *obviously* nigh, and that it was going to hurt.

All attempts at measuring the depth of the Hole had met with failure. Objects tossed in disappeared forever. Sonar and laser and various beams shot down the Hole simply diffused, from all the dust, after a few miles. Sensors lowered into the void broke their cables at about fourteen miles—twice the depth of the deepest manmade hole. At that depth the atmosphere in the Hole was still air, the walls still sheer rock, the temperature about 190°F. The diameter and circularity remained the same all the way down.

Jerry "Mercy Me" Kincannon, the first and only chthononaut, was lowered into the Hole on a cable reinforced with Madagascar orb-spider silk. At eight miles, it broke, sending Jerry toward the center of the Earth and the cable bungeeing back to the surface. But it hadn't actually broken; the end had clearly been cut. This pleased the Hellists.

Jerry's last meal had been chicken tikka masala and Hole Holes.

Back in Evanston, Suttling House, to the Johns' great surprise, started to come together. It was now under the management of Orisse LeClaire, a chef they'd hired before they left for Texas. She looked like Lena Olin as Ingrid imagined Lena Olin had looked at seventeen. At first Ingrid was sure that David had hired this slice of Belgian cheesecake as a vicarious bodiment of Megan, but Ingrid was beginning to feel that David had, perhaps, simply hired who he thought was the best person for the job.

Orisse had added to the menu a basic but perfect steak au poivre, a two-bean cassoulet with lamb sausage, and David's chicken tikka masala, the recipe for which David had finagled from the owner of the best Indian stall at Heathrow Airport. And doughnut holes. For the first time in its short history, reservations were required to dine at Suttling House.

And Hole Holes was starting to do well too. Within six months the Johns had grossed nearly $200,000, mostly from doughnut holes. Every day the Brink's truck would circle the entire bustling perimeter, collecting all the cash and receipts from the vendors. When Ingrid noticed that their bag of cash was as big as anyone else's, she became begrudgingly pleased. Slowly, she began to feel tiny flakes of resentment toward her husband crack off and float away. Between longueurs of anger, Ingrid and David occasionally smiled, and even kissed once, a self-conscious buss over the Hobart. Ingrid declined an invitation from the manager of Quescaisje?, three doors to the east, to join him in a toke

of hash and a quick screw, something she would have strongly considered a year before.

From the very beginning, the Hole (for reasons the Hellists attributed to the infectious clouds of decadence, greed, and gluttony emerging from it) had attracted increasingly tony restaurateurs. The first vendor had not been a restaurateur but a flintknapper; the second guy sold bottled water and Lone Star longnecks out of a pair of Igloo coolers perched on the tailgate of his pickup; the third was a *raspado* vendor; and the fourth was a mobile franchise of the forward-thinking Lillocq, a Gault-Millau-17 restaurant near Marseille whose owner was well known for gambling, travel, risky business ventures, and hypermania. He was the Bugsy Siegel of West Texas.

Of the original three vendors, only the flintknapper remained, selling arrowheads at ten bucks apiece and repelling aggressive six-digit offers from Russians and Bahrainis to buy out his space. Lillocq persisted in a state of constant profit, working haute sorcery on local game, dairy, vegetables, and Gulf seafood. Even though there were plenty of ordinary vendors—most of whose spaces had been acquired by lottery, like Hole Holes—the Hole quickly became a Parnassus not just for scientists and doomsayers, but for wealthy gourmands, restaurant critics, foodie tourists, and culinary spies.

And oenophiles. Early on, a woman, Jolene Taft, had bought Lot 44 to set up Alcool 13%, the Hole's only wine coach. She brought along two of her uncles to help out, as well as her only daughter, ten-year-old Mindy. Of the 151 vendors, the wine coach, according to the *Wall Street Journal*, was the most profitable of all, with a first-year gross of nearly $3 million. Part of its success rose from the publicity surrounding an extraordinary act of superstitious excess: a Russian apartment-building manager of more-than-modest means walked up and purchased the most expensive bottle in Alcool's cellar—a 1945 Romanée-Conti with uninterrupted provenance and ullage to the cork—and, without notice or ceremony, lobbed the $80,000 bottle over the fifteen-foot

Hurricane fence and into the Hole. It was rumored that he'd then driven to Athens, Ohio, and bought a Powerball ticket worth $90 million, though the truth was that he'd merely returned to St. Petersburg $80,000 poorer, and resumed apartment managing.

Jolene had screamed and fainted at the sight of the valuable bottle tumbling in its trajectory, but she quickly found that her love of wine did not exceed her desire for money, and so was not compunct in selling other rare and costly bottles that no one but the Hole would drink. Her daughter, Mindy, loved the thrill and flagrant naughtiness of big spenders flaunting in the name of idolatry.

One afternoon, when a mournful Upper East Sider named Sue Penning bought a '99 Muller-Scharzhof Riesling, sneaked past the Hole's gatekeeper, Brody Kremer, and jumped into the Hole with her bottle, Mindy, who had been watching, screamed and ran off into the scrub oak until she came up against the perimeter fence, where she sat crying, thinking of the mournful woman's yellow and blue skirt as it came up over her head as she fell.

Mindy stood up and followed the perimeter fence for nearly an hour until she happened to come across another girl, the first person near her age that she'd seen there. The girl was busy attending to a tiny ranch made of kebab skewers in whose one corral could be found three sturdy horny toads.

"What're you gonna do with those?" said Mindy.

"I'm gonna take them home to live in the tub."

"Where do you live?"

"Right there, see that ginger-bread house?"

"What do you sell?"

"My parents sell dough-nut holes and stuff."

"Oh, that's you? Those're good. You should come over to my house. I have a man-sion."

The next day, more holes opened up. One appeared in the geographic center of the Caucasus (235 yards across); another in the Northern Territory, Australia, about 150 miles north-northeast of Alice Springs (688 yards across); and another in the interior of French Guiana, only five miles from the coast (41 yards across). There were also hundreds of reports of smaller holes—a foot across or less—opening up in basements and driveways and landing strips and battlefields and World Heritage sites.

Most newsworthy was the four-and-a-half-mile-across hole that yawned open in Finland, swallowing up part of the town of Kemijärvi and many of its 8,300 residents.

The U.S. Geological Survey estimated that in that one day, .00000001 percent of the Earth's surface was punctured—that was the word employed, *punctured*, in all its laughable imprecision—by forces that it said *had* to be geologic in nature.

After that, new holes appeared every day, all over the world, sometimes claiming villages, sometimes city blocks, sometimes just sand dunes or Antarctic coal or windy steppe. At least the seas weren't draining away; for whatever reason, holes were a landlubberly phenomenon. But this was cold comfort to a reducing world: it was clear that eventually everyone on the planet would either disappear into a big hole, or become marooned between holes. Fewer and fewer people came to visit the premier Hole.

Maryellen spent as much time as she could at Mindy's. Maryellen was glad for Mindy because Maryellen had gotten lonely, and none of her old friends wanted to come out and visit.

After the first year at the Hole, Maryellen's parents had sold the camper and built their little gingerbready house on a small leased lot only a few yards away from their business. Late one night, Maryellen slipped out of the window in her room and began to jog around to the other side of the Hole, where Alcool 13% was, taking care to stay out of the bright cones of the many streetlights. Finally, out of breath, Maryellen snuck up to Mindy's house—a huge New Orleans–style double-gallery painted deep purple—and tossed a few caliche pebbles up at Mindy's window. Presently Mindy emerged through a side door, a Burgundy bottle in one hand.

"C'mon," said Mindy. "I know where to get in."

"In what?"

"C'mon!"

"Is that full?"

"Come. *On!*"

The two girls ran. After a few minutes, Mindy stopped. She crouched down next to one wall of Arcimboldo, which had just gotten its second Michelin star and was doing well in spite of the paucity of customers, and motioned for Maryellen to crouch down beside her.

"It's right there," said Mindy. "See? Where it's bent up a little? We can get under."

"Under the *fence*? No way!"

"Way."

"We'll fall in! It goes to hell!"

"We won't fall in, and my great-uncle says it probably only goes to the Moho discontinuity, about thirty miles down."

"No!"

"So stay here, I don't care. I'll drink this by myself."

Mindy began to sneak toward the fence.

"Wait!" Maryellen hissed.

Mindy ignored her. She reached the brightly lit fence, lay down in the dirt, and worked her skinny body through a breach just large enough for a ten-year-old.

Maryellen raced up and crawled through too.

Mindy walked right up to the Hole and sat down, her feet dangling in the void, as though she were perched on the edge of a swimming pool, stirring the water with her toes. Maryellen could hardly see her; the fence was floodlit, but it was nearly dark at the Hole. A few yards away was a stone memorial to poor Jerry Kincannon, the only person to die exploring the Hole.

Maryellen looked up. Here came Brody Kremer. His job was to slowly circle the walkway outside the fence in a golf cart, looking for trouble and nipping at vermouth. There was no way he'd be able to see Mindy, but he'd see Maryellen for sure if she stayed where she was. So she got down on all fours and began to crawl slowly toward her friend. When she reached the edge, she peered over. Just black. With surgical care, she sat on the edge like Mindy. The lip was sharp and uniform, and cut into the backs of her knees.

"Just imagine you're sitting on a normal chair," said Mindy. "You've never just fallen off a chair onto the floor, right? Unless somebody pushed you?"

"Yeah, I guess."

"Okay? Good. Hold this bottle."

"Don't even fake-push me, Melinda Lacey Taft."

"I won't! God!"

Mindy reached inside her overalls and came up with a corkscrew and two plastic wineglasses. She gave the glasses to Maryellen and took the bottle back. And with a grace that suggested Mindy had opened bottles before, she pulled the cork.

"Want me to smell it?" said Maryellen.

"No, that's for losers who don't know anything. Hold those out."

Mindy poured both glasses about a third full, and took one.

"This cost three hundred dollars. My mom'll murder me if she finds out I took it. Swirl it around."

"I thought they just did that on TV."

"No, that's real. Now sniff the wine. Really stick your nose in there."

"It smells burny. And kind of like Lucky Charms."

"Now hold it up to the light."

The act of twisting a half turn caused Maryellen's bottom to shift a quarter inch toward the Hole. She screamed a short, powerful chirp, flailed, and spilled her wine in the dirt.

"Omigod! Omigod!" said Maryellen, backing up from the Hole.

"Jerk! We're gonna be in so much effing trouble if Brody catches us!"

"Omigod!"

"Shh! Now come back, it's cool, be cool, Maryellen."

Maryellen slowly returned. Mindy refilled her glass.

"Okay?"

"Yeah."

"Now. Drink a little, but don't swallow. Let it warm up in your mouth—that's when all the flavors come out. Then swallow when it starts to burn. See? What's it taste like?"

"It doesn't taste like grapes."

"It should taste like cherries and tobacco and wet stones and pitch and ... wait ... uh, I think violets. Or, wait, figs. No. I forget."

"It makes me pucker."

"That's something in the wine."

"No duh."

"So do you like it?"

"I guess."

"Here's some more. We'll drink it all and throw the bottle and glasses in the Hole."

"We shouldn't throw anything in there, that's what my mommy says."

"Well, your mommy doesn't have all the facts."

"What facts?"

"We're all gonna have to leave soon."

"Why?"

"Trash."

"Huh?"

"That's what they decided to use the Hole for. All the trash in the world, including nuclear bombs."

"So why would we have to leave?"

"You really think people wanna eat and smell old garbage at the same time?"

"Can I have some more?"

"Don't drink it too fast or you'll get alcoholism."

"I feel tingly, like my head's falling asleep."

"Then you're doing it right."

"It feels nice."

Mindy and Maryellen lay back in the dirt.

"You know that the devil cut Jerry Kincannon's cord, right?" said Maryellen, hoping to impress her older friend with her knowledge of the world of adult tragedy.

"No, he probably cut it himself."

"But they said no one could cut through that cord, so it must have been the devil, who can cut anything he wants to."

"He probably saw something that made him go crazy, like huge white bugs or something. That's all that happened."

The perimeter lights shut down. It was one in the morning. Above, the stars slowly resolved. It was easy to imagine them as holes too, poking through the walls of the universe into something even bigger, something bright, someplace where Jerry Kincannon could live in happiness.

"Look, I can pour it right in my mouth," said Mindy, holding the bottle with both hands.

But Maryellen was asleep.

The reportage of worldwide hole news had fallen upon the shoulders of one man, a Louisianan named Harry Bell, whose gruff Morgan City drawl now sputtered from an old AM/FM radio high on a shelf inside Hole Holes, where Ingrid was mincing garlic and ginger in one corner, and David was standing over a scorched saucepan on a wavery flame at the old gas stove. The Johns were making a chicken tikka masala for Den Pinchbeck, the flintknapper, who had lately lost his family when a hole opened up in nearby Rosewild. Ingrid, who wanted to make the dish special somehow, recalled the scene in *GoodFellas* where a character sliced garlic with a razor blade into very thin slices, thereby more thoroughly investing the cooking oil with garlickiness. While Harry Bell reported that 5 percent of the planet was now officially pocked with

supernatural cavities, and that thirty-two million people had gone missing, Ingrid honed and stropped her knife until the slivers of garlic fell in delicate, virtually transparent ovals.

David, who felt that the commercially prepared ghee they usually used wasn't quite nutty enough to pique a proper masala, stood over the old stove clarifying a few ounces of butter for Den's meal. Once he had skimmed off the last of the milk solids, he heated up the clarified butter in a cast-iron skillet. Ingrid looked at her husband, who gave a nod, then scraped in her palette of sliced, see-through garlic. They leaned over the skillet, and together waited the few exquisite seconds until it was time to put in the ginger.

Brody Kremer gave the Johns a ride over to Den's place, but Den wasn't there. His camper was gone, as were his collection of potted succulents and his bag of raw flint. All that remained was the low range of tiny flint chips that formed a rampart around where his folding chair used to be.

Late summer, early evening, a cool breeze picking up, the tandoor just about the right temperature, David loaded it up with skewered, boneless chunks of nilgai rump meat—chickens had lately been impossible to come by—while Mindy and Maryellen fried thirty-one doughnut holes that they planned to assemble into a pyramid, douse in powdered sugar, top with a candle, and present to Ingrid for her birthday, her thirty-first, and third at the Hole. Three vendors had closed up in the past week—Arcimboldo, Fahrah's Kebab Outpost, and Quescaisje? (oh, how the the owner had begged, for three years, on his knees, for just one night with Ingrid)—and now there were only ten of the original 151 left. Alcool 13% still had good connections and access to a private plane, and so they always had great bottles ready to be bought and pitched into the Genuine Original Hole by hysterical persons with increasingly desperate needs to sate the devil, or whatever it was that had perforated the Earth

with now billions of holes, one of them nearly 400 miles across, and another 300 yarder only a quarter mile from the Johns' home. But most Hole businesses had closed up quite a while ago for lack of ingredients, or customers, or both. The infrastructure—the bank, medical center, security, plumbing—had mostly all collapsed, and electricity was intermittent. The Johns needed very little—onions, garlic, spices, rice, ginger, meat, butter, yogurt, flour, sugar, oil, water, a few herbs—but even this modest cupboard was becoming more and more difficult to fill.

The nilgai meat came out of the tandoor. David mixed it into his Heathrow Airport masala and cooked it for a bit over the open fire behind the house. In the distance a hollow, sucking *hoomf* sounded, the bawl of a new hole being born. A quarter of the Earth's surface was now welled with them. An ingenious nuclear-powered machine had been invented in Korea that was able to crawl down into small holes, a yard or so across, and return after a deep plumbing. One had traveled 2,992 miles, reporting uniform circularity and diameter the whole way down—a geological impossibility: magmatic guts should have percolated and overcome the machine. Whatever death the Earth faced, it was a consummate, antiscientific, ineluctable one, and soon to come.

David served nilgai tikka masala to his wife and daughter, and to Mindy and her mother and the remaining great-uncle (the other had disappeared a year before). Jolene opened two bottles of '89 Haut-Brion, and poured healthy glasses for the adults, and thimblefuls for the girls. David and Ingrid, sitting back-to-back to keep warm against the growing chill, ate the Indian stew and drank the good wine. Jolene tossed a comforter over the couple and said, "No naughtiness now," while David and Ingrid giggled underneath. Jolene began to sing "Happy Birthday" as Maryellen and Mindy came out with the doughnut-hole cake. They had found a single candle somewhere. Ingrid lifted up an edge of the comforter to see. The mesa wind picked up, cool and aggressive, but the candle didn't go out. 🅛🅟

SUSTAINABILITY

BY NINA BAI

CAPRICORN
(The Sea Goat)

YOUR GREAT WORRY is that no one knows what you are, sea goat. Perhaps your mother grazed too closely to Superfund sites, but regardless of how you came to be, you're not alone. After the Deepwater Horizon oil spill, Gulf fishermen found eyeless shrimp and crabs with holes in their shells. In southern Idaho where a mining company had been dumping selenium into local creeks, trout spawned baby fish with two heads and contorted fins. In the Potomac River, male smallmouth bass grew eggs in their testes because of estrogen in the water. Everywhere, aquatic life soaks in the hormones, antidepressants, pesticides, sewage, oil, oil dispersants, and industrial effluents we flush down the drain. The good news: science may yet find a use for you. James Murray, an animal scientist at the University of California, Davis, recently created transgenic goats whose milk helps prevent diarrhea, a leading cause of childhood death around the world.

AQUARIUS
(The Water Bearer)

YOU FEEL UNAPPRECIATED. You're worn out: your natural abundance and resilience can only go so far. For a brief spell after the Cuyahoga River in Ohio caught fire in 1969 (not the first time), Americans paid attention to water, bringing forth the Clean Water Act and the Environmental Protection Agency. But the collective concern has moved on. "The biggest problem in the States is that we here have gotten so good at collecting, treating, and transporting water that we don't think about it anymore. We take it for granted," says Alex Prud'homme, author of the *The Ripple Effect: The Fate of Freshwater in the Twenty-First Century*. Those around you remain willfully ignorant of water quality and unwilling to regulate it. Nobody seems to know how much it takes out of you to produce things: three liters of water for one liter of bottled water, 634 gallons for an eight-ounce steak, 919 gallons for a pair of blue jeans. Every year, the average American uses 751,777 gallons of water. Sadly, things will likely get a lot worse for you before they improve.

HOROSCOPES

ILLUSTRATIONS BY
LOREN PURCELL

THESE ARE UNCERTAIN TIMES for you, and your luck will depend on being in the right place at the right time. Avoid international travel if possible. According to Paul Greenberg, author of *Four Fish*, "There's a disconnect between people worrying about the oceans and how nations manage their fish." The fate of a fish very much depends on who owns the water it swims in. Along the coastlines of the U.S., Australia, New Zealand, and Iceland, better fisheries are rebuilding fish stocks. In developing countries, overfishing and problems of poorly managed aquaculture—from the overuse of antibiotics to destruction of mangrove forests—are common. Life is especially dangerous if you're traveling the high seas. A bluefin tuna crossing the Atlantic, for example, travels through multiple jurisdictions with competing regulations, creating a tragedy-of-the-commons scenario.

PISCES
(The Fish)

BEWARE ALLURING STRANGERS and social climbers. You're looking for love in all the wrong places. Now is the time to stick close to your own. Adapted for snowy, steep terrain, the Sierra Nevada bighorn sheep is one of several subspecies of bighorn sheep native to the American West. John Muir admiringly called them "animal mountaineers." But an unfortunate meeting of New World bighorn sheep and domesticated European sheep spelled disaster for the former. Domestic sheep blithely carry pathogens that cause deadly pneumonia in wild sheep, killing off hundreds of bighorn in some years. In 2000, with only about a hundred animals remaining, the Sierra Nevada bighorn sheep was given endangered status by the federal government. A major conservation challenge is simply keeping wild and domestic sheep away from each other, says Tom Stephenson, who leads the California Department of Fish and Game's Sierra Nevada Bighorn Sheep Recovery Program. If you're a wild ram searching for females during rut (breeding season), you'll be tempted to approach a domestic ewe, but beware of what you might bring

ARIES
(The Ram)

home. "It wouldn't be as much of a problem if a ram came down to domestic sheep and died," Stephenson says, "but they go back to their native herd and readily spread the diseases." Conservation efforts have boosted the Sierra Nevada bighorn population to more than 400 animals, but your recovery is far from guaranteed.

TAURUS
(The Bull)

YOU'VE DEVELOPED a bad reputation as a global-warming gasbag, but you can't be blamed. You're just digesting your food. If humans can't take the heat, let them eat kangaroo. Every year, American cattle expel a collective 5.5 million metric tons of methane, a greenhouse gas that's twenty times as effective as CO_2 at trapping heat. The country's staggering one hundred million cattle—both grain- and grass-fed—are responsible for 20 percent of the country's methane emissions. Researchers are testing various gas relievers, including diets of flaxseed and alfalfa, omega-3 supplements, and vaccines that reduce rumen (foregut) microbes. Australian microbiologists are peering into kangaroo rumens, trying to learn why they emit far less methane and hoping to transfer the conditions to cow rumens. The United Nations ranks livestock as more dangerous than all planes, trains, and automobiles combined in global-warming impact. But the blame doesn't rest entirely on your gut. Your friends need to do their part, too. When farms store dung and urine in sludgy, liquid form, it decomposes into yet more methane and acid-rain-causing ammonia.

GEMINI
(The Twins)

DOUBLE THE BABIES, double the fun, you'd think. But things are starting to get a bit crowded. You're feeling healthy and strong, but that could pose a problem, too. Too many babies and longer life expectancy are the twin forces driving overpopulation. In much of South Asia and Africa, populations are growing rapidly, exacerbating malnutrition, depleting natural resources, and incurring higher mortality and morbidity. India alone contributes 22 percent to worldwide population growth. Women in Mali, Niger, and Uganda have an average of six children. Population explosions can overcrowd urban areas and fuel civil unrest. "People are getting on flimsy boats on the Mediterranean and the Red Sea, taking desperate measures to migrate out," says Joseph Chamie, former director of the United Nations Populations Division and former director of research at the Center for Migration Studies. On the flip side, the populations of Japan, South Korea, Spain, and Italy are shrinking and aging. By 2035, nearly a third of Japanese, Germans, and Italians will be over the age of sixty-five. In Japan, sales of adult diapers already exceed sales of the baby variety. You'd do well to be prepared for the future. Countries where birth rates are slow can expect economic stagnation and rising social and healthcare costs for the elderly. These countries should consider welcoming more migrants. Meanwhile, countries with surging populations should provide better access to birth control.

THINGS ARE LOOKING up for you blue crabs. As the most valuable catch in the Chesapeake Bay, your stock has been exhausted for decades. But help is finally on the way. After your population dropped to its lowest ever—around 300 million in the mid-1990s—interstate political wrangling stopped winter dredging practices that were scooping up vulnerable egg-laden females. Thanks to these regulations, there are eight hundred million of you now. "Things are looking pretty good—the signs are there that the recovery will continue," says Thomas Miller, director of the Chesapeake Biological Laboratory at the University of Maryland Center for Environmental Science. And while cold-loving lobsters are terrified of global warming, you're the kind of crustacean who doesn't mind warmer waters. The one wrinkle to look out for is a growing gender imbalance. Choosy females, you mate once in a lifetime during a critical one- or two-day window. A successful meeting with a male means several million fertilized eggs, while a missed connection means a genetic dead end. With relatively fewer males around to play the mating game, Miller advises lady crabs "to be sure you get your mate early on."

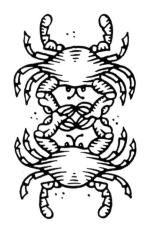

CANCER
(The Crab)

IT'S TIME TO face the facts: you're a wild animal and need your own space. Humans and their dim-witted livestock are all up in your habitat; it's a relationship that's bound to be toxic. Stay away—they're not to be trusted. Though you once roamed from Greece to India, you're now found almost exclusively in eastern and southern Africa. An estimated 30,000 to 35,000 wild lions survive, with dramatic declines attributed to conflict with expanding human communities. Lions attack and eat more than a hundred people a year in Tanzania. In retaliation, people are lacing half-eaten carcasses with insecticide or rat poison, killing lions who return for seconds. Ironically, your salvation may be in captivity. "It's naïve to think that lions will persist anywhere where it's not fenced," says Craig Packer of the Lion Research Center, who has studied lions for more than thirty years. "Imagine if lions were wandering in Central Park and ate a couple of people every month—people wouldn't put up with that. It's terrible," he says. "It's easy to understand why people wouldn't want to live with them."

LEO
(The Lion)

YOU'RE BEAUTIFUL, STRONG, intelligent, and productive. Have the confidence to go it alone. Many plant species have evolved the ability to produce seeds asexually, a process known as apomixis, in which the egg cell keeps two sets of its own chromosomes and eschews contributions by sperm cells. Sex introduces variety, but it's hit or miss. "Basically you're already adapted to an environment, you're thriving. If you undertook sexual reproduction you'd be producing a lot of variability," says Peggy Ozias-Akins, a professor of horticulture at the University of Georgia. By studying naturally apomictic plants, researchers hope to introduce asexual reproduction into crop plants like millet, corn, and sorghum. Plant breeders expend considerable time and energy creating hybrids with the most desirable combination of traits, but that hybrid vigor is inevitably lost in the genetic reshuffling of plant sex. Sex complicates everything.

VIRGO
(The Virgin Maiden)

LIBRA
(The Scale)

YOU FEEL OUT of balance, overloaded. And with good reason: today, two thirds of Americans are overweight and more than a third are obese, and the rest of the world is following our example. Education about healthy eating is not the problem, says Marion Nestle, professor of nutrition, food studies, and public health at New York University. "Everybody knows what they're supposed to eat, but nobody does it." Changes to U.S. farm policies in the 1970s encouraged overproduction of crops like corn and soybeans, lowering prices and flooding the market with cheap, calorie-dense foods that were aggressively promoted by multinational corporations. The 1980s and '90s saw sharp increases in body weight. Today, young children are developing type-2 diabetes and people younger than twenty are suffering from strokes. Grassroots political movements that lead to government regulations, like New York City's soda cap, may be the most effective way of curbing the epidemic, Nestle says. In the meantime, hold tight and brace yourself for even heavier loads to come.

SCORPIO
(The Scorpion)

FROM DESERTS TO rain forests, you've conquered every continent except Antarctica, and yet you still get no respect. It may be your defensiveness, or your sharp sting. They say branding is everything. You share the arthropod phylum with insects and crustaceans. Consider an image revamp as "land lobster." You're a highly nutritious and sustainable food choice, says David Gracer, a self-described professional zealot of entomophagy. "No matter what it is you're talking about, insects require less of it," says Gracer—less feed, water, time, space, machinery, and petroleum than vertebrate livestock. Bugs also carry a lower disease risk than cows and chickens, and less saturated fat than most meat. You're packed with calcium, phosphorus, and vitamins. Gracer, who has eaten scorpion on many occasions, will admit you're an acquired taste, with a strong, fishy flavor "like the inside of a sneaker on a hot day." In a good way.

SAGITTARIUS
(The Archer)

MODERATION IS CRUCIAL. You love the thrill of the hunt, but don't shoot out of season. Eat what you kill. During the Great Depression, FDR signed the Federal Aid in Wildlife Restoration Act, which included an 11 percent excise tax on guns and ammunition that would go toward funding wildlife conservation. Seventy-five years later, the Federal Aid in Wildlife Restoration Act—which now also taxes fishing gear and bows and arrows—has provided more than $12 billion to various conservation and research programs, resurrecting species such as the white-tailed deer and the wild turkey. It may seem ironic, but you share many of the same goals as conservationists: habitat protection and maintenance of sustainable populations season after season. Now is a good time to make unexpected new friends. More urbanites have turned to killing their own meat for environmental and ethical reasons. It's possible to see hunting game for food as an extension of the sustainable-food movement—something that will become more vital if agricultural systems collapse. **LP**

THE APOCALYPSE IS UPON US

A collaborative vision of how it all ends.

ARTWORK CREATED THEN DESTROYED BY
ROBYN O'NEIL, JOSH COCHRAN,
AND SCOTT TEPLIN

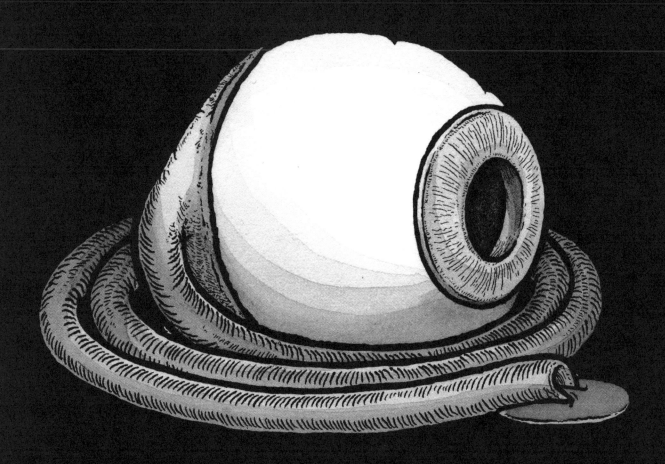

This is it. The end. We've spent half the magazine preparing you for it, and now it's here. From here on out, you're on your own.

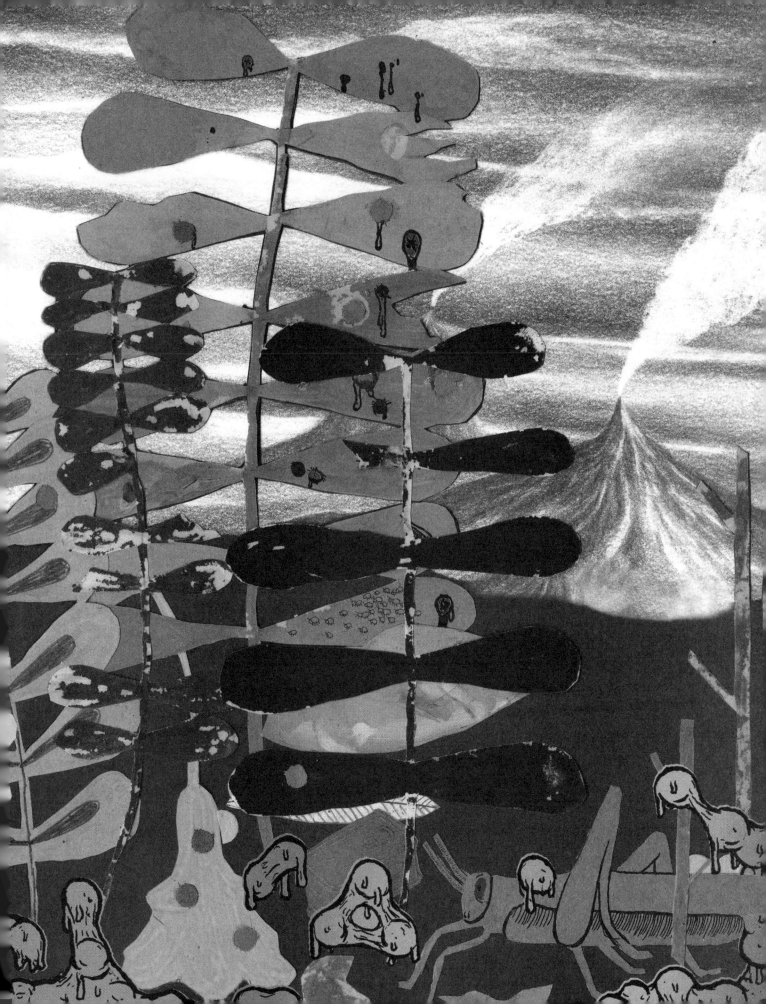

colored by Marissa Louise

thebrooklynkitchen.com

TED NUGENT

ROCK LEGEND, GREAT WHITE BUFFALO

Laurie Woolever: Do you believe that we are on the precipice of an apocalyptic or Armageddon-like event? What would be your plans for survival, specifically when it comes to having enough food?

I do not believe we are about to experience the endgame—not at all. Though the recent presidential election proves there is an unprecedented population of soulless fools hell-bent on the scourge of self-inflicted dependency, I have undying confidence in the powerful good of America and mankind winning over the bad and ugly, no matter how ridiculous things seem to be.

I have always had fire extinguishers even though I have never had a fire. I am a Boy Scout, and I am always prepared. Since graduating from high school, I've made certain that all my homes and properties have unlimited renewable wildlife, water, fish, forests, nut and fruit trees, and everything necessary to remain totally independent.

**INTERVIEW BY LAURIE WOOLEVER
ILLUSTRATIONS BY CHRIS VON SZOMBATHY**

As far as firepower goes, I can best be described as a guns-and-ammo glutton.

If you could have only one gun during the apocalypse, what would it be?

I would never settle for one gun, but just for Q&A's sake, I would cling to my Colt M16/M4 full-auto 5.56 mm, fully equipped with quick-detachable open sights and optics and various accoutrements to enhance functionality and accuracy. Because it is chambered for the ubiquitous 5.56 (.223) round, given our ridiculous ammo supply, ammo would never be a problem. It is well suited for both self-defense and taking game. My entire family is most proficient with its use and necessary tactics.

Can you describe the person who is most ideally suited for survival after the apocalypse?

He is a man's man with an indefatigable gung-ho warrior attitude and spirit; he is six foot two inches and approximately 215 pounds of muscle and sinew; he is an expert with all weaponry; a deadly stealthy hunter/fisher/trapper/killer; he has an uncanny, higher level of awareness that comes from being clean and sober and from bowhunting his entire life; he can work with his hands and most common tools; he is unlimitedly creative and can improvise, adapt, and overcome with the best of them; and he is known for writing the ultimate love song of all time. Think "Wang Dang Sweet Poontang."

What would be (or is) in your apocalypse-preparedness pantry?

We have always had them. We rotate canned goods, rice, flour, canned meats, vegetables, and fruits; plus the basics of salt, pepper, seasonings, sugar, powdered and canned milk products, and stacks of various freeze-dried foodstuffs and prepared meals. We even have a stash of military MREs.

Do you have pets in the Nugent household? Under what circumstances could you be forced to eat them?

The thought is most discomfiting, since we seriously love our dogs and stupid cat. In a life-and-death situation, for the survival of my beloved family, we would certainly improvise, adapt, and overcome with whatever it would take to live. I suppose the old gray cat, M, would have to become sweet-and-sour pussy in a pinch. After all, anybody who has eaten at a Chinese restaurant has already eaten such yummy meat, I assure you.

Imagine all the meat's gone. What is your next source of protein? What are your thoughts on cannibalism?

It is inconceivable that we would run out of meat on our home grounds, as there is an unending supply of annually

renewable wildlife that would feed us forever. My thoughts on cannibalism are the same as all civilized people's: sheer disgust. That said, we are all well aware of those numerous documented cases where that most powerful survival instinct has kicked in under dire circumstances, and such last-ditch decisions have indeed saved lives. When in doubt, we would whip it out.

What type of human (young, old, fit and lean, fat and lazy, urban or rural or suburban dweller) would make the best eating, and why?

They say that human fat is quite sweet, and with all the disgusting obesity slobbering amok, I would probably go for the fat girls if push came to shove. Again, I would prefer squirrel meat right down to the last rodent before resorting to such repugnant moves.

In the wake of a catastrophic event, what's the best thing a gun-owning individual/household can to do ensure their long-term survival? What about a non-gun-owning household?

A non-gun-owning household won't have to worry much, because they will be killed off rather quickly. Unarmed and helpless is, after all, unarmed and helpless—a pathetic condition of soulless, irresponsible stupidity. For those of us who value life and are armed to the teeth, the joys of aim-small-miss-small marksmanship discipline have prepared us for all of life's ugly criminality, and we would simply implement the basic proven tactics of securing the perimeter and double-tapping center mass. Only a fool would choose to be outgunned. **LP**

LEFT BEHIND

TEXT, PHOTOS, & ROT BY
BENJAMIN WOLFE

A FIELD GUIDE TO POST-RAPTURE ROT

A brilliant flash of light, followed by a world-swallowing cloud of darkness. In a second, it's all over. Believers float merrily toward heaven; sinners and pagans are absorbed into the ground. There's not even enough time to whisper a quick "I told you so" to your heathen neighbors. It's the rapture!

Heathens or not, neither the chosen nor the damned will have the chance to finish their meals. Tasting menus at the world's best restaurants will be arrested midcourse, leaving freshly prepared dishes untouched and vulnerable on their tables.

In the weeks and months following, molds will reign as new kings. Released from the oppression of humanity's need to preserve, molds will devour the food we leave behind.

On the pages that follow, you'll meet the moldy overlords of the post-rapture world. Signature restaurant dishes were prepared and left to rot, providing a fuzzy, mushy, and putrid glimpse of the mycological paradise that will rise in our wake.

PORK BUNS
Momofuku

No surprise here: fuzz showed up to liberally blanket David Chang's buns. Their starchy surface functioned as the ideal landing pad for mold spores. One of the most abundant molds to make its home on the buns was *Scopulariopsis*. This mold created brown splotches on the buns, similar to the spots it creates on old wheels of naturally aged cheeses. *Scopulariopsis* has a knack for growing in diverse habitats all over the world—not just pork buns—from marine sponges to the hooves of horses.

food preparation by **SCOTT JONES**

OYSTERS AND PEARLS

Per Se and the French Laundry

This is a spoilage microbe's wet dream come true—a microbial waterpark perfect for molds that love high-moisture environments. A pile of caviar, oysters, eggs, and cream provides plenty of proteins and fat to fuel a lush carpet of mold. An interesting color flip happens with this dish as it rots: the pile of caviar goes from brown to yellow, and the sabayon goes from yellow to brown.

MUCOR: The mass of dark brown mold is *Mucor*, a mold that loves it wet! Tiny little balls on the ends of the dark brown threads (hyphae) are packets of spores that allow this mold to disperse itself easily. *Mucor* is a close cousin to the fungus used to make tempeh (*Rhizopus*) and is often the mold that forms a beard on your neglected strawberries.

GEOTRICHUM (or *Galactomyces*, depending on which mycologist you talk to): Much of the frosty white fuzz that quickly covered the surface of this dish is *Geotrichum candidum*. This is the same fungus that creates the brainlike, undulating rinds of French goat cheeses such as Chevrot, Charolais, and Bucheron. *Geotrichum* is what turned the mound of caviar from dark brown to yellow.

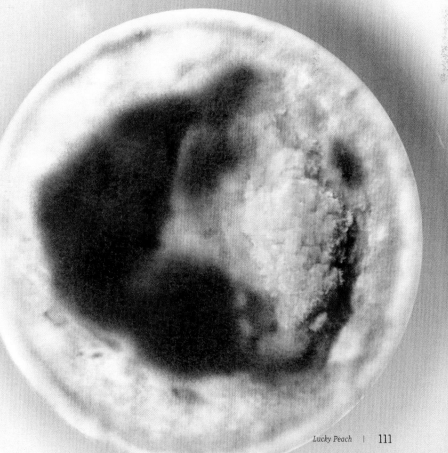

RADISHES IN A POT
Noma

This radish pot is a mixed bag for molds. The delicious dollop of herb cream at the bottom of the pot would ordinarily make any mold go wild. But the layer of malt "soil," baked for many hours, has sealed that cream off from the outside world, rendering the pot's interior ultimately unfavorable for mold growth. Rotting radishes, "planted" in the soil, serve as a conduit between the aboveground air and the creamy belowground.

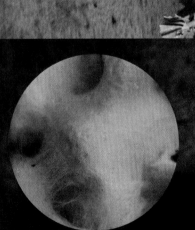

FUSARIUM: *Fusarium equiseti* frequently grows on plants and likely got to the rot party on the radish bus.

Fusarium molds have a complicated relationship with humans. Some species produce potent mycotoxins and can be devastating pathogens of plants (*Fusarium graminearum* and *Fusarium oxysporum*). Others can infect your toenails (*Fusarium oxysporum* and *Fusarium solani*). Yet some *Fusarium* species are beneficial to humans. The rinds of many stinky washed-rind cheeses are held together with *Fusarium domesticum*. Lovers of the fake meat mycoprotein Quorn are eating the guts of *Fusarium venenatum*.

BONE MARROW SALAD
St. John

Fergus Henderson's signature dish is bone dry, making it a challenging environment for molds. Only the parsley and marrow inside the bones provide moisture. But some xerophilic (dry-loving) molds can tolerate these low-moisture environments. Using the limited moisture in the air, they break down starches and proteins in the bread as an energy source. As this dish rotted, the fungi built a fuzzy network of hyphae that extended outward from the bread and covered the entire plate.

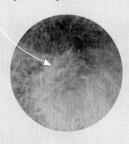

NEUROSPORA: *Neurospora crassa* is a bread-loving mold that is happily rotting this dish. Scientists originally described this fungus in the 1840s when it was found to be a contaminant in French bakeries. It later became a lab rat for the field of genetics and led to a Nobel Prize in 1958. In Indonesia, this mold is used to make a fermented food cake called red oncom that is similar to tempeh. The hyphae of this fungus are initially white, but can turn bright orange when it produces spores.

PENICILLIUM: *Penicillium*, another bread-loving mold, quickly took up residence on the grilled bread. Although it's maligned as a cause of food spoilage around the world, *Penicillium* also provides us with delicious cheese (the fuzz on the outside of Brie and the blue veins on the inside of blue cheese) and spurred the antibiotic revolution in medicine.

Chances are you've grown *Penicillium*—if you've ever let bread sit around long enough to turn blue-green.

The fuzzy white bits are the hyphae of *Penicillium*; the spores (called conidia) it produces are the blue, green, and gray colors that we often associate with moldy food. Just as different species of plants have different flower colors, different species of *Penicillium* have different spore colors. The two different shades of blue on this dish are evidence of two different species of *Penicillium* dining together.

PRUNE-STUFFED GNOCCHI
No. 9 Park

Barbara Lynch's prune-stuffed gnoc-chi, slathered in foie gras butter, are incredibly savory and pleasantly sweet. But what's decadent for humans turns out to be terrible for molds. The high fat content of the sauce inhibits the growth of molds, just as rubbing lard on curing meats inhibits mold growth. This dish was not, however, impervious to rot. The skillful work of yeasts—the single-celled relatives of the molds— turned the pasta into a pile of mush.

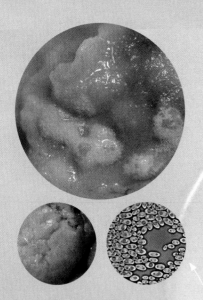

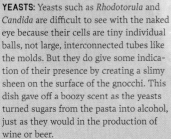

YEASTS: Yeasts such as *Rhodotorula* and *Candida* are difficult to see with the naked eye because their cells are tiny individual balls, not large, interconnected tubes like the molds. But they do give some indication of their presence by creating a slimy sheen on the surface of the gnocchi. This dish gave off a boozy scent as the yeasts turned sugars from the pasta into alcohol, just as they would in the production of wine or beer.

GOAT CHEESE SALAD

Chez Panisse

Some bacteriologists out there will probably be peeved at my mold-centric view of post-rapture rot. I've focused on the molds, because they are the most obvious rotters. Bacteria tend to be the attention whores of the microbiology world. It's fun to ignore them for a change. But bacteria are also playing an important role in the decomposition of these signature dishes.

This is best exemplified in Chez Panisse's baked goat cheese. The goat cheese became moldy with white *Penicillium* hyphae. (Many aged cheeses are coated with a layer of *Penicillium*.)

The most surprising and disgusting part of this rotting dish is the brown pile of mush that formed as the lettuce rotted. If you've ever kept a container of spring mix in your fridge too long, you've probably seen something similar. This mush is largely a result of *Pseudomonas* bacteria. These bacteria are naturally found growing in low abundance on fresh lettuce leaves. When left to their own devices, they break apart the components of the leaves using powerful enzymes. In the process, they produce rancid, brown mush. *Pseudomonas fluorescens*, the most abundant mush-maker in this dish, produces a compound that is fluorescent under a black light— try this with your rotted spring mix! Perfect for a post-rapture rot rave. LP

ROAST CHICKEN,
2034
BY MAGNUS NILSSON

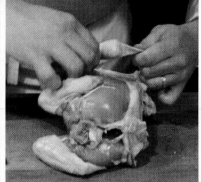

Last summer, on an unending drive over lurching Polish dirt roads, I turned to my backseat companion and asked—primarily to distract myself from carsickness—"Magnus, could you strip a chicken of all its skin and flesh, meat-glue pork in its place, reattach the skin, and roast it?"

"Sure. We could do it."

"Cool."

We left it at that. But a few weeks later, he e-mailed: "When are we making the Frankenchicken? Come visit Fäviken."

I said that I wished I could, but I couldn't justify a trip to his restaurant in central Sweden just to cook a joke-dish. He told me not to worry about it. The next e-mail I received was from Sweden's tourism office. At Magnus's urging, they'd arranged for a series of planes to ferry me from San Francisco to Fäviken, where men are free to turn a bird into a pig.

In the ramp-up to our encounter, we mused over the possible applications of the frankenchicken. We imagined the year 2034: Industrial poultry has continued down its dismal trajectory to a nadir of inedible toxicity. It is banned, worldwide, from consumption. But roast chicken still holds a place in the hearts of sentimental diners, and chefs—obliging folks that they are—must devise workarounds. Thus, Roast Chicken, 2034. Poultry made safe for consumption by removing the poultry.

When I reached Fäviken's doorstep, I was blindsided by how incomprehensibly pristine the place is. It's safe to assume that no industrial chicken or pig had ever crossed the restaurant's threshhold. Magnus had no idea what to make of the meat glue. He sifted it onto the poultry carcass like powdered sugar onto beignets, warning that we probably shouldn't breathe it in.

The chicken collapsed into a pile of meat, and a very convincing pig-bird rose in its place. We faced our creation. The Frankenchicken had emerged from the joke-swamp into fully formed reality. Thinking about what was under the skin made me a bit uneasy, like rewatching *Lethal Weapon* now knowing what Mel Gibson is like. Later, when we ate the thing, it was disconcertingly tasty. —**CHRIS YING**

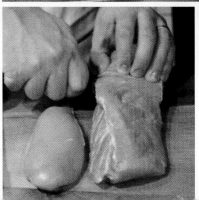

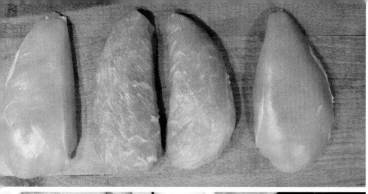

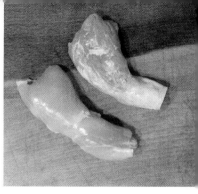

ROAST CHICKEN, 2034
aka The Frankenbird

1	very low-quality chicken
1 kg	sirloin of pork (Danish industrial pig for its beautiful color)
1	tenderloin of pork, industrial quality
1 big bag	Activa RM transglutaminase (meat glue)
+	staple gun
+	medical gauze

1. Place your bird on a big, stable cutting board, breast-side down. Cut through the skin from the neck down to the Pope's nose, following the back bone.

2. Undress the bird as though you were peeling off a really tight unitard. Be extra careful around the wing joints and thighs where it is easy to break the skin. Reserve the skin.

3. Now carefully cut the meat away from the bones. Pay attention not to slice into the different parts; you want to keep the breasts and legs intact to act as templates for later meat sculpting. When done, the carcass should be quite clean of any chicken meat.

4. Place a piece of sirloin next to one of the chicken breasts, positioning it carefully so that the meat fibers are aligned in the same direction on both pieces of meat. Carve a breast piece out of the pork, and set aside. Repeat with the other breast/sirloin.

5. Open the tenderloin of pork into a flat 10-mm-thick layer with a very sharp knife. Keep all the pork sinew attached to give the correct texture and mouthfeel of chicken leg meat.

6. Cut the tenderloin fillet across into two pieces and powder with meat glue. Shape each piece so that it is somewhat triangular, with the narrow end corresponding to the lower part of the chicken thigh and the leg. Use the deboned chicken parts to guide you in achieving the correct shape and thickness.

8. Powder the cavities that used to hold the breast meat liberally with meat glue and fit the pork-made breast replicas into them. Affix with gauze and staples.

7. Take a piece of "thigh meat" and fix it to the bone structure by rolling the more narrow part around the leg and putting the

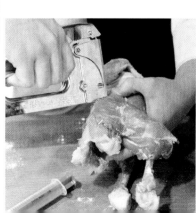

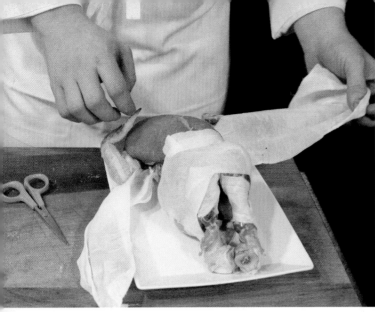

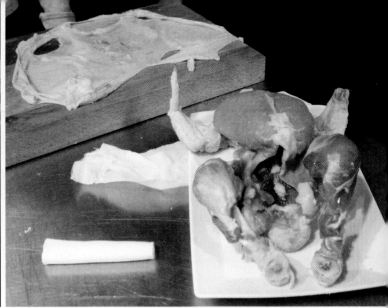

wider part flat against the pelvis of the animal. Fix with gauze and plenty of staples, repeat on the opposite side. Refrigerate for a few hours.

9. Remove all the gauze from the bird and pry out as many staples as you can. The meat should be secured to the carcass now. Trim any loose bits with a pair of sharp scissors.

10. Powder the carcass with even more meat glue and redress the frankenchicken with its reserved chicken-skin

unitard. Fix the sliced back with staples. Leave to set in the refrigerator overnight before cooking.

11. Roast like you would a normal chicken. (I started ours in an oven, before transferring it to a pan on the stove with a bit of garlic. Then I basted it with butter until it was well browned and smelled disturbingly alluring.) Serve with brussels sprouts, roasted potatoes, cream sauce, and a nice mature Bordeaux.

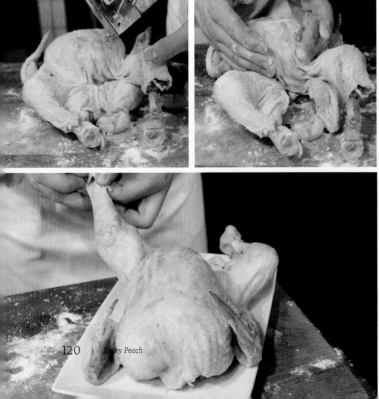

Final-dish photo and recipe by **MAGNUS NILSSON**
Other photos by **JAMI WITEK**
With thanks to **DARK RYE**

ATTENTION ALL HUMANS

IF YOU CAN MAKE IT TO BOB SMITH'S ZOMBIE TRAINING COMPOUND, YOU CAN SURVIVE

SIGN UP TODAY AND LEAVE WITH YOUR VERY OWN GLOW-IN-THE-DARK CROWBAR TO KEEP THE CREATURES OF THE NIGHT AT BAY!

Ten years ago, Bob Smith was just a chef. Then he decided to get serious about zombie defense. His friends mocked him. Well, who's laughing now?

Bob Smith is now the world's premier zombie-survivalist expert, helping hundreds of survivors defend themselves against the undead. Bob's weekend-long programs include invaluable lessons about how to turn ordinary household objects into zombie-stopping artillery:

- Turn your sporting equipment into life-saving tools with **frozen paintballs**!
- A **baseball bat** will have zombies home running away from your property!
- Bullets are more valuable than gold bullion. **Crossbows will save you!**
- EACH WEEKEND ENDS WITH A MEAL AT **BS-60**, Bob's under-the-radar Westchester County tavern! The **pepperoni pizza** is a can't-miss!

YUM!

THE **ONLY** ZOMBIE SCHOOL WITH **LIVE** ZOMBIES!

save yourself at

BOBSMITHSZOMBIECAMP.COM

BRAAAAAIIIINNSSS
RECIPES FROM THE ZOMBIE DINER

Listen, you may have been turned into a zombie, but that doesn't mean you can't appreciate a decent meal. Of course brains are on the menu. But before you grab the first fleeing person you see and start slurping, consider this: brains have been a favorite ingredient of human chefs for centuries, and we've gotten pretty good at making them tasty. Here are three elegant yet simple dishes that even an undead knucklehead like you can make. —GENEVIEVE KO

Zombie photo and illustrations by **LINDSAY MOUND**

BRAIN-CRUSTED RACK OF LAMB

From Jean-Georges Vongerichten | *Makes 12 servings*

| Blanch and peel brains | → | Make brain crust | → | Brown lamb | → | Drape brain crust; broil | → | Rest; serve |

When Jean-Georges Vongerichten opened his flagship restaurant Jean Georges in 1997, this simple dish amazed diners, who couldn't figure out how a simple herb-crusted lamb chop could taste so rich. The secret? Brains! Vongerichten learned to appreciate the peculiar and intense creaminess of brains as a child growing up in Alsace. His grandmother would sauté them in butter, with capers, lemon, and parsley, and serve them with potatoes.

Years later, Vongerichten snuck brains onto his menu in the form of a crunchy-creamy crust for lamb, punctuated with the garlicky bite of mustard garlic, a wild foraged herb. This dish hasn't been on the Jean Georges menu for years, but with sufficient demand from the zombie set, it could make a reappearance. If it does, it will be served on a spotless porcelain plate atop a pressed white tablecloth under a polished cloche. Try not to drool on the silver, okay? —**GENEVIEVE KO**

INGREDIENTS

2½ lbs	veal brains
5 cloves	garlic
1 bunch	flat-leaf parsley, leaves picked
½ lb	garlic mustard greens, trimmed and chopped (or substitute more garlic if you can't find these)
¾ lb	butter, softened
1½ T	Dijon mustard
+	kosher salt
+	freshly ground black pepper
+	panko crumbs
6	lamb racks, frenched
+	grapeseed oil

1 **Fill a large bowl with ice water**, and bring a large pot of water to a boil. Add the brains and poach for 4 minutes. Drain and chill completely in the ice water. Once cool, drain the brains again, and peel off the exterior membrane; reserve.

2 **Pulse the garlic, parsley, and garlic mustard greens** in a food processor until very, very finely chopped. Add the butter and continue to pulse until well mixed.

3 **Add the mustard**, poached brains, and a generous pinch of salt and pepper. Pulse a few times to combine; don't overmix, the texture should be just this side of smooth.

4 **Add a handful of panko** to the food processor and pulse. Keep adding panko and pulsing until the mixture becomes tacky and spreadable. Line a half-sheet pan with plastic wrap and spread the brain-butter on top in an even ¼-inch-thick layer. Cover with plastic wrap and refrigerate until firm.

5 **Use a spatula to pry the chilled butter** out of the pan. Slice the brain crust into rectangles the same size as the tops of the racks of lamb. Return to the refrigerator.

6 **Generously season each rack** of lamb with salt and pepper. Heat a skillet over medium-high heat, and add a thin layer of oil, then add a lamb rack, bone side up. Cook until golden brown, 4 to 5 minutes, then turn and brown the other side. Transfer to a baking sheet; reserve. Repeat for remaining racks.

Preheat a salamander or broiler, with the oven rack 6" from the heat source.

7 **Arrange a rectangle of brain crust** over the rib-side of each rack. Slide under the broiler (in the pan or on the baking sheet). Cook until the meat is medium-rare (about 130°F) and the brain layer is golden brown.

If you want to save your bones from blackening like those in the photo, wrap the bones in aluminum foil before sliding the racks under the broiler. Otherwise, leave the foil out and go for the apocalyptic charred-remains look.

8 **Rest the racks for a few minutes**, then slice them into two-rib chops. Note that the crust will slip off the meat with the barest provocation. You have to be super delicate when moving the rack whilst broiling, and when slicing the chops.

*Use an offset spatula to peel the brain-butter from the pan (**step 5**).*

*Slice the brain crust to be the same size as the surface of the lamb (**step 5**).*

*Be gentle when cooking and slicing the lamb. The crust falls off easily (**steps 7 and 8**).*

GOAT MAGHAZ FRY ON TOAST POINTS

From Hemant Mathur of Tulsi | *Makes 6 servings*

Poach brains → Make sauce → Simmer brains → Assemble and serve

At home on Sundays, Hemant Mathur might make this dish along with some roti—stuffing the brains in the warm bread for a dribble-down-the-hand wrap. At his restaurant, Tulsi, he serves it with toast points, dainty triangles with the brains spooned on top. But that's really the only difference. The seasoning mix is the same one his mom makes in northern India, where *maghaz* (brain) dishes like this are popular among Muslim

Mughals. Mutton brains are the offal of choice.

You can use the thinking organ of another animal if you like, but the key is taming the brains. The combination of milk and spices takes the offaly edge off. Mathur then builds on that base, stewing the brains with more spices and then finishing them with fresh garam masala. The dish makes for a nice canapé—just enough to whet your appetite for more braaaaaiinnsss. —**GENEVIEVE KO**

INGREDIENTS

1 C	whole milk
1 C	water
1 t	black peppercorns
3 pods	green cardamom
1 pod	black cardamom
1	bay leaf
¼ t	fennel seeds
+	salt
½ lb	goat brains
2 T	canola oil
1	medium onion, diced
1" piece	fresh ginger, peeled and finely chopped
2	fresh green chilies, stemmed and finely chopped
¼ t	turmeric powder
¼ t	red chili powder
2	small tomatoes, finely chopped
¼ t	garam masala
6 slices	good bread, crusts removed
2 T	cilantro, chopped
+	kosher salt, to taste

1   **In a small pot**, bring the milk, water, peppercorns, cardamoms, bay leaf, fennel, and a pinch of salt to a boil. Slice the goat brains into ½" pieces, and poach in the milk until firm, about 3 minutes. Drain through a sieve, then pick out the whole spices. Reserve the brains.

2   **Add the oil to a heavy skillet** over medium-high heat. Add the onion and ginger, and cook, stirring frequently, until the onions are well browned. Add the chilies and continue to cook, stirring, for 30 seconds. Add the turmeric and chili powder. Give it all a quick stir and cook for 30 more seconds.

3   **Add the tomatoes and cook**, stirring occasionally, until they're soft and mushy. Add the poached goat brains, raise the heat to high, and cook for 3 more minutes. Taste and add salt if needed. Sprinkle the garam masala on top and remove from the heat.

4   **Cut the bread slices into triangles, and toast**. Dollop a spoonful of brain on top of each toast triangle, sprinkle with cilantro, and serve immediately.

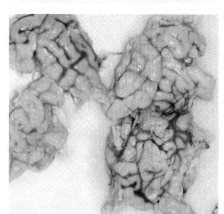

*Brains, once poached and strained, are firmer and lighter in color (**step 1**).*

*Simmer the tomatoes until soft, then add the goat brains (**step 3**).*

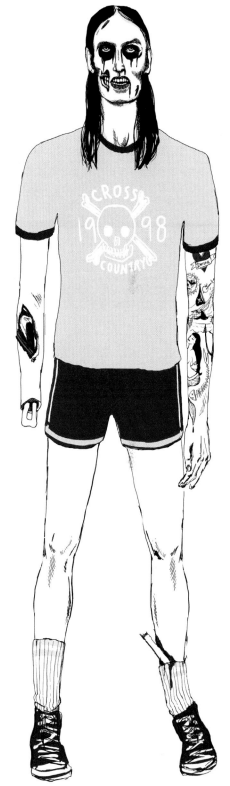

CALF'S BRAINS FRITTO MISTO

From Gabrielle Hamilton of Prune | *Makes 10–12 servings*

| Soak brains overnight | → | Blanch and peel | → | Coat and fry | → | Make brown butter | → | Serve |

Soaking brains in milk draws out the little bit of remaining blood left in the mass of membrane and deposits white, inoffensive milk in its place. Inexplicably, I always skip this step with sweetbreads, another organ generally treated the same way. I guess I don't mind the occasional dark brown capillary in my fried thymus glands. But somehow, spots in brains—it's too much. The idea of eating them is inherently challenging. They are challengingly custardy. I don't like to burden them with the third challenge of unsightly dark blood threads. The milk helps with a consistent white complexion.

When they rarely happen to be sold, brains are sold whole, with the brain stem attached. Keep them intact through the soaking and poaching steps if possible. Once they have been poached and shocked, split them apart at the natural cleavage and discard the creamy soft white stem. If your butcher sells you single lobes (pre-split

brains) you don't need to worry about that step.

Brains can be breaded and fried like anything else. But before that, there's one final brain-specific step: pulling off the chalky, thin membrane that encases the lobes. It is a gentle endeavor. I tug at a sturdy point with the tip of a paring knife and then gently pull the rest of the way with my fingertips. Pulling off a nice, clean, largish sheet feels very rewarding, though the process does call to mind some mixture of cleaning up fresh cobwebs and lifting oozy chewing gum from a scorching sidewalk.

I tested this recipe using approximately 4 pounds of brains, the minimum my butcher shop would sell me since they have to be specially ordered. Four pounds yielded between 10 and 12 useable portions, though I'll note that unlike other foods, I'm only ever good for one plate of brains—they're almost too custardy and rich.

—GABRIELLE HAMILTON

INGREDIENTS	
4 lbs	calf's brains
+	milk
+	salt
1½ C	all-purpose flour
2–3	large eggs, beaten
2 C	panko bread crumbs
3	gala apples, cored and cut in eighths
12	cippolini onions, peeled but left whole
+	neutral oil for deep frying
½ lb	butter
½ C	salt-packed capers, rinsed
+	lemon wedges

*Browning butter in a stainless steel pan makes it easier to see the color difference (**step 6**).*

*The brains, apples, and onions should all cook in about the same time (**step 5**).*

1 Soak calf's brains in milk overnight in refrigerator. (Try to get a full 24-hour soak.) Discard the pink-tinged milk and rinse the brains well.

2 Poach the brains in gently simmering, generously salted water until firm and set, about 5 minutes. Carefully transfer to an ice-water bath to stop the cooking. Drain and transfer to a wire rack.

3 Gently peel the very thin membrane off the brains in one sheet as best as possible. Use the sharp tip of a paring knife to get started. This feels like peeling a fresh, sticky cobweb off the lobe.

4 Dredge the brains in flour, pat off excess, then dip in the eggs, and coat with the panko. Set on a wire rack. Commit the apples and onions to the same process.

5 Deep fry the brains, apples, and onions at 350°F at the same time, but work in batches as needed to avoid crowding the pan. Everything will cook approximately evenly and should be ready in between 4 and 5 minutes. Drain on a wire rack or a stack of coffee filters. Season with salt.

6 In a stainless steel pan over medium heat, cook the butter until fragrant, foamy, and brown. Pour into a ramekin with the rinsed capers.

7 Arrange the fried food on butcher or parchment paper on a plate and serve with the caper brown butter and lemon chunks.

ARMAEGGDON

While there are a great many foodstuffs from Pennsylvania's breadbasket that will undoubtedly endure the apocalypse, the question really is: which of them will sate the hunger of the discerning survivor? My bet is on red beet eggs. They are pickled, of course, and ubiquitous. Menacingly rosy jars of them haunt the back bars or counters next to the cash register of many of the greater Lancaster area's finer and not-so-fine establishments. Most are graced by a gray halo of dust that says, "I've been here since the seventies, and I'll be here after you're gone." No doubt that's the attitude you'll want to take into the looming zombie/robot/alien wars, and with their mix of fortifying protein and piquant beetiness, these eggs will help keep your fighting spirits high!
—MARK IBOLD

INGREDIENTS

1 dozen	eggs, hard-boiled and peeled
12-oz jar	pickled red beets (in their liquid)
1 C	vinegar
1 C	water
3 T	sugar
1 T	salt

1 **Put the hard-boiled eggs into a glass jar.** If you want the End Times to be fancy, you could tuck some tarragon and a clove of garlic in there, too.

2 **Heat the beets, vinegar, water, sugar, and salt until just boiling.** Dump over the eggs. Put into the fridge (or the coldest area of the cave you are hiding out in) for a few days and they should be ready to eat. The longer the eggs stay in the liquid, the more colorful they will be when cut in half.

BEEKEEPER

CHASE EMMONS, BROOKLYN GRANGE

Jamie Feldmar: Where do beehives occur in nature? Where can I look for wild honey?

Honeybees are not native to North America. The Pilgrims brought them from Europe, but the climate is not ideal here. Selectively bred, bees can make it through cold weather, but in general, winters tend to kill them off. In the South, that's not a problem. But after the apocalypse, there probably wouldn't be many bees north of the freeze line in North America.

Out in the wild, the usual place you find them is not in a hive, it's in structures, like a wall cavity in a building or house. They'll set up hives in hollowed-out tree trunks, or any hole in the wall. You find them inside of drywall all the time. Also rafters and ceilings. Sometimes you find them in old tree limbs, but that's comparatively rare. You might find a hive hanging in an abandoned warehouse, or inside air ducts in office buildings. It doesn't matter what we view the space as; to bees, any sheltered, dark place is a good place for a hive. Recently, we found some in the Brooklyn Navy Yard living in defunct fire hydrants: a perfect armored area for them.

**INTERVIEW BY JAMIE FELDMAR
ILLUSTRATIONS BY HONEY BEASLEY**

Bees really like spaces like that—big cavities with small entrances.

Say I've found bees living in a wall. What do I need in order to steal their honey?

The first step is to fashion some sort of protection. Indigenous tribes in Africa who've been dealing with bees for thousands of years climb up natural rope ladders in loincloths, with bunches of smoky twigs crammed in their waistbands to ward off bees. But mere mortals will want to protect themselves. If you're digging through their hive, the bees will want to sting you. Even a good pair of jeans will protect you from getting stung. It's a matter of covering all exposed skin with something thick: jeans, sweatshirt, two regular shirts, and some sort of headgear. You could use plastic bags for gloves. (In the apocalypse, there will probably be plenty of plastic bags floating around. You'll probably want to use two or three layers.)

Headgear is tricky: how do you fashion a veil so you can manipulate the bees and not get tagged in the face? You can't cover your face in duct tape. Ideally you want a wide-brimmed hat that hangs out a few inches in front and behind your head so you can hang some sort of veil from it. A sombrero is perfect. Or even two wire hangers, bent into a circle, and one across your head to balance it.

For the veil, you need something see-through and breathable, like a piece of a screen door or window. Cut a circle of screen that's about eight inches by three feet, then curl it into a hoop, and attach it to the brim of your hat. Make sure it drapes down to your shoulders so you're totally covered.

Another option is a five-gallon pail, if you're able to cut a porthole for your face, and cover that with screen. That's not bad: a bucket on your head with a screen on it.

How would you go about actually harvesting the honey?

The basics are: (1) Protect yourself from getting stung, (2) Grab everything, and (3) Run like hell. (That is, of course, if you're unconcerned with leaving the colony intact, and you're just interested in pillaging the hive for the honey the way a bear would.)

The cool thing about honeycomb is it's its own container. So if you carefully cut out the honeycomb, you don't have to have a container to carry it. What you need, though, are tools to pry into the cavity the bees are in: a crowbar, or big stone, or anything like that. If the bees are in a wall, and you've found their entrance, you've still got to demolish the wall to get to the honey.

You also need a smoke source—a fire. When you rip open the wall, you want to have your smoke source already going. In small quantities, smoke calms the bees, and in large quantities, it actually works as crowd dispersal. You essentially smoke the bees out so they'll fly away.

You can create a smoker with an old soda can. It's like making a weed pipe out of a Coke can. Punch a hole in the bottom, and stuff it with twigs or leaves or paper. Light that on fire, and blow into the bottom, so smoke comes out the top. You want mostly smoke, and not too much flame. You don't want to light yourself on fire.

Before you rip open the wall, squirt some smoke into the bees' entrance hole to calm

them down. Once the wall's torn open, grab the honeycomb, then wave the smoke all over the comb so they'll leave. Smoke the crap out of it. Shake the comb so the bees fall off and fly away. Just cut everything out and take it with you. The bees will attack you when you do this. That's why you have armor.

Flee the scene. The smoke will also help cover your tracks. The bees won't follow you.

Is that legal?

Laws probably won't apply after the end of civilization, but until then, and in general, you should not go messing around with wild beehives. Sure, it's legal to do whatever you want with bees that set up in your walls or on your property, and you definitely should not allow them to remain as it can cause huge property damage. But calling a seasoned beekeeper who deals with removing colonies is the way to go since the bees get to be relocated and live in regular hives.

An alternative to raiding the hive and destroying it is only taking what you need and making sure not to remove the queen. That way, you'll have a renewable source of food in a relatively secure location. Heck, then you'll have honey to trade, which I bet would be seriously valuable in Bartertown, postapocalypse.

How would you go about leaving the colony to ensure a steady supply?

The basic approach would be to identify big chunks of comb that only contain capped honey, or mostly capped honey. It's usually easy to tell the difference between capped honey and capped brood. The capped honey cells are somewhat translucent or cloudy colored and flush with the rest of the comb, while capped brood cells are chalky white and somewhat puckered kind of like bubble wrap. You'll want to use some sort of blade to cut out sections of the honeycomb carefully so that you don't

crush any bees or drop it and crush bees. It's actually a bit difficult to spot the queen, even for the experienced. So your best bet is to cut out some honeycomb, then firmly shake it over the other comb or inside the cavity where the colony is. You'll shake off most of the bees and the queen if she happens to be on it. She does not fly, so there's no risk of her flying away. (If you want to identify her, she is bigger than the rest and has a long, skinny abdomen. Problem is that drones (male bees) are also pretty big. Drones have very big heads and eyes, while the queen has a normal-sized head on a long, skinny body.) If the queen is killed, it's not the end of the world. If it is spring-summer, the colony will most likely raise a new one, especially if it's a big, healthy colony.

Another way is to identify the piece of honeycomb you want to cut out and then use your smoking device to drive the bees off of it. Be careful not to set fire to anything, or burn bees. Just use it like riot control and drive the bees off just the section you've targeted.

Seal up the hole you cut in the wall or tree trunk or whatever, while still leaving their original entrance unblocked, and there you go. You can keep coming back for more.

If you are in a winter climate and you want to make sure the bees will survive until spring, don't take too much. It's their only food supply for the winter months. In spring-midsummer you can take a good amount and it's fine; they'll replace it.

What can I expect from the wild honey?

You'll find huge sheets of honeycomb, laden with bees and larvae and eggs and honey. It's not all honey. You'll find honey in certain spots and baby bees and larvae and eggs in other spots.

You can just eat the entire honeycomb, including the larvae. They're these little white worm grubby things. It sounds gross, but the reason bears attack hives isn't because of the honey. The bears want the larvae, because they're a great source of protein, and the honey

is like dressing. Eat the whole damn thing. There aren't any stingers on the larvae. You can just mash it up, the whole comb, in a gourd (or whatever postapocalyptic container you find). It's a superfood! You could essentially subsist for months on just that. It's really comprehensive. Each little grub has a chunk of bee fat, the simple carbs from the honey, and even some protein from pollen. Google "Honeyman Tribe." There's a documentary on this Ethiopian tribe that lives on the stuff.

If you'd rather not eat the honey, use the screen from your veil as a filter. Create a colander, and hang it over a bucket or any kind of container. Using your hands, just crush the crap outta the honeycomb and dump it into the filter. The wax and grubs will stay on top, and the honey will just drip through the filter.

What benefits would there be to harvesting honey in a post-apocalyptic world?

The thing about honey is that it's an antiseptic and has infinite shelf life if sealed and kept in a cool, dark environment. They've found edible honey in 5,000-year-old Egyptian tombs. So as long as you keep your honey in a sealed, cool area—even like an old plastic bag to keep critters out, or put it in some secure place away from raccoons and bugs—it will last many years.

But it's not just the honey that's antiseptic. You can gnaw the comb and not worry about any contamination. The propolis—what bees use to caulk their holes up—has antiviral properties. Egyptian and Roman battlefield medics all carried honey to dress their wounds.

Would bees survive the apocalypse?

Nature always survives. You could nuke the planet, and in a million years, you'd never know we were here. Barring something super catastrophic—an asteroid, maybe—bees would be fine. **LP**

JELLYFISH
THE ONLY SEAFOOD LEFT

Much of Thailand already cooks from something akin to an apocalyptic pantry. I recently visited my mother's hometown, Mae Chan—a small town in Chiang Rai, about half an hour from the Burmese border—where people have been eating the same way for a long time. Theirs is a simple subsistence diet based around what's available and what keeps well without refrigeration: fish sauce, rice powder, simple herbs and vegetables, fermented shrimp paste, fermented fish, dried powdered fish, homemade chili paste, instant noodles, and whatever creatures you might find in small rivers and rice paddies— eel, frogs, mudfish, catfish, and my favorite, *mang da* (waterbugs). If the end-of-the-world thing really does happen, I figure Thais are in a pretty decent position to ride it out in style.

Once overfishing has emptied the oceans of all their delicious stuff, what we'll have left is tons of jellyfish, which, when it comes to protein—let's be honest—is never anyone's first pick. Even in parts of Thailand that traditionally eat jellyfish, I don't think jellyfish is ever a first choice. It's always like, "Oh, the river prawns are really great. The crab is really good." But no one ever really says, "Oh, this jellyfish is really amazing." Jellyfish kind of sucks. It doesn't have great flavor. It's just matter.

Nevertheless, we know how to eat it. It's not one of those ingredients that might benefit from the chef cliché of non-intervention, as in, "I want to showcase nature's bounty and let jellyfish shine on its own." For jellyfish to taste good, you actually have to do something to it. In my case, that means shamelessly overseasoning.

**—KRIS YENBAMROONG,
NIGHT + MARKET**

Note: If you know how to butcher jellyfish, feel free to break them down yourself. For my recipes, I use jellyfish that you find in plastic packets at the Japanese supermarket. The jellyfish bells are already sliced, then packaged in salt water. Make sure you get the plain, unmarinated kind.

JELLYFISH TOM SAEP

Isan-style soup | *Makes 4 servings*

Make chicken stock → Toast/bruise aromatics → Poach jellyfish → Garnish and serve

Tom saep is a soup that's funky and fairly spicy, made from super simple ingredients. It's a traditional Isan (northeastern) dish, and it's normally made with mushrooms or beef innards, like tripe. Think of this as a Thai menudo.

When shopping for fermented fish (*pla ra*), do not buy the kind that says "creamy version" on the label. Gouramy and mud fish are good ways to go, and Pantainorasingh is a good brand. All the different brands have their own vibes, but are generally decent across the board. It's just a matter of tasting a bunch and figuring out what you like.

—**KRIS YENBAMROONG**

INGREDIENTS	
1	chicken, or a couple pounds of legs or wings
6 qts	water
1 C + 1 T	fish sauce
+	white pepper
1	large shallot, peeled and coarsely chopped
2 T	lemongrass, sliced on a bias
3-4	kaffir lime leaves
1 T	galangal, minced
2-3 T	bird's eye chilies, sliced into ½" lengths
1.5 T	lime juice
1 T	juice from a jar of fermented fish (pla ra)*
1 T	sugar
1 C	packaged jellyfish, cut into bite-sized pieces
4	dried arbol or bird's eye chilies
2	scallions, cut into ½" lengths
1 T	cilantro, both leaves and stems, coarsely chopped

You can season the soup with liquid from the pla ra jar, or make nam pla ra.

1 **Thai chicken stock** is really just chicken bones and fish sauce boiled together. Thai seasonings are typically intense, so the simplest of stocks is preferable. What we're aiming for is liquid that's just more flavorful than water.

Put the chicken in the largest stockpot you own, and fill with water. Add 1 C fish sauce for every 6 quarts of water. Shake some white pepper in there, too. Let it boil for a couple minutes before turning down the heat. Skim if you're feeling French. Let it simmer for a half-hour if you're in a rush; an hour is better; longer is better still. We keep ours simmering on the burner all day and add water to replenish as we go and fish sauce as needed. Strain. You'll end up with more stock than you need. Cool the remainder and store in the fridge.

2 **Toast shallot, lemongrass, lime leaves, galangal, and sliced chilies** in a dry wok on low heat, until fragrant and everything is black around the edges. Bruise the aromatics using a mortar and pestle. You don't want to work it too much. Isan food can be sort of unpolished. Place the bruised aromatics into your serving vessel—ideally one of those Thai hot pots with a chimney and room for a Sterno can underneath—along with the lime juice.

3 **Boil 1 T fish sauce, 2 qts stock, sugar, and 1 T of the juice** from a jar of pla ra (see note below) in a soup pot. Drop in the jellyfish pieces and boil for 2 minutes. Pour the jellyfish and stock into the hot pot on top of the toasted/bruised aromatics and lime juice.

4 **Fry the arbol (or bird's eye) chilies** for a few seconds in a splash of oil, then drain and cool them. Crack into large pieces. Scatter the scallions, cilantro, and cracked chilies into the soup. Light the Sterno and serve!

* **Tom saep is traditionally fortified with *nam pla ra*,** a potent sauce that's hard to track down. It's made from fermented fish (nam pla), which is made by salting freshwater fish and adding rice, then letting it stew in big earthenware vessels for six months to a year. The result is less frightening than you might think. It smells like a really overripe French cheese that got left out overnight in a fish market. In a good way! Really.

As instructed in this recipe, you can season the soup with a spoonful or two of the cloudy juice that comes in a jar of pla ra. But if you're ever, say, running a Thai pop-up restaurant in Los Angeles and want to make the real deal, start by dumping all the contents of a jar of pla ra into a pot. There will be murky liquid and pieces of fish. Simmer it on low heat, adding water a bit at a time until you've roughly doubled the volume. Stir occasionally so it doesn't stick (it kind of will anyway) and when all the fish is disintegrated, strain the fish juice back into the jar. Discard the solid nasty. The liquid is *nam pla ra*. Refrigerated, it'll last longer than you need it.

JELLYFISH YAM KAO TOD

Crispy rice salad | Makes 3 servings

| Prep chili jam | → | Make curry paste | → | Fry crispy rice | → | Season jellyfish | → | Toss salad; serve |

Central Thailand, near the water, is where I've seen jellyfish eaten. *Yams* are one of the main preparations there: spicy, seafood-heavy salads served at room temperature. It's always sour, salty, spicy, a tiny bit sweet, loaded with a lot of herbs. Because the yam is crunchy and sour and spicy, it's really good beer food. You'll probably want to be drinking anyway, to take your mind off the apocalypse and the fact that you're stuck eating jellyfish.

"Yam" is a noun that can also be used as a verb, as in, "I'm gonna yam the hell out of those foraged mushrooms." This dish is a take on a dish called *yam nam kao tod*—a salad of crispy rice, fermented pork, chili, and some other stuff. I'm just replacing the pork with jellyfish.

The crispy rice here is basically homemade Thai-seasoned Rice Krispies. At the end of the world, you could totally substitute the Rice Krispies from your pantry.

—**KRIS YENBAMROONG**

INGREDIENTS

½ C	packaged jellyfish, cut into bite-sized pieces and boiled in Thai chicken stock (see Jellyfish Tom Saep recipe, page 136), and strained
1 T	sugar
2 T	fish sauce
2 T	lime juice
2 T	sliced red onion
2 T	scallions, coarsely chopped
2 T	thinly sliced bird's eye chilies
2 T (or more)	cilantro, leaves and stems, coarsely chopped
3 leaves	sawtooth leaves, cut into 1" lengths
1 C	crispy rice or Rice Krispies
¼ C	roasted peanuts
1	3" piece of ginger, peeled, finely julienned

CHILI JAM (NAM PRIK)

1½ T	tamarind paste
+	oil for frying
2	dried large chili pods (about 5" long and 1½" wide)
½ C	sliced shallots
½ C	sliced garlic
+	salt

RED CURRY PASTE

½ C	minced galangal
¼ C	kaffir lime zest
½ C	lemongrass
½ T	*gapi* (fermented shrimp paste)
½ C	dried arbol chili
½ C	garlic
¼ C	shallots
+	salt
+	veggie oil

CRISPY RICE

3 C	cooked jasmine rice
5 T	red curry paste
+	rice flour
+	oil for frying

Poach the jellyfish in Thai chicken broth. There's a recipe on page 137.

*Just-fried dried-out rice (**step 4**). Add more curry paste to make yours redder!*

1 For chili jam, start by making tamarind water. Take a small hunk of tamarind paste—it will be sold in bricks at any halfway respectable Southeast-Asian grocery—and put it in a small bowl. Cover with boiling water. Once the water has cooled enough to handle, massage the lump into a gloopy slurry and strain out the solids. Boom: tamarind water.

2 Next, deep-fry the chilies, garlic, and shallots separately. Use the same oil for all. Fry the chilies first and quickly—just for 5-10 seconds to activate the aromas. They will char very fast and you don't want that because it'll make the nam prik bitter. I fuck that up sometimes if I'm not paying attention. The way to compensate for it is to add 2 or 3 times the amount of tamarind water later. Fry the shallots next, until golden and soft; remove them with a slotted spoon; then fry the garlic, just until golden.

Put everything in a food processor and blend with enough tamarind water till it's jammy. Once you get the consistency of jam, season it with a little more tamarind water and salt. The nam prik should be sweet and sour, with underlying saltiness. This will make more than you need for this recipe. Nam prik is the base for a lot of things, including tom yum soup. I put it in a great deal of what I make, to round things out and make dishes more cohesive.

3 For the red curry paste: you're looking for blender-ish smoothness out of a mortar and pestle. Mince everything as finely as possible, then start the pounding with the galangal, because it's the most resistant to being broken down. Imagine ginger made out of rock—that's what galangal is like. Throw in a pinch of salt to help. Next, add the lime zest and pound, then the lemongrass. You want to create as smooth a purée as possible. Add the shrimp paste and pound to incorporate. The shrimp paste is what anchors this whole thing. Add chilies and pound. Add garlic and pound. Add shallots and pound. When it's all incorporated and as fine as it's going to get, fry it up in a small pan with a bit of vegetable oil over low heat.

Both the curry paste and chili jam will keep for weeks, if not longer, and can be used in any number of dishes. Slather the curry on some chicken and grill it. Spike soups with either the paste or jam. Both work in all kinds of applications, and can be profitably substituted for the canned and jarred versions that everybody relies on.

4 **Turn rice into crispy rice**. Take cooked jasmine rice—some people use sticky rice but I use jasmine—and marinate it with red curry paste. It should be faintly red—redder even than in the accompanying picture. (Sorry. —*Ed.*) Try to separate it as much as possible into individual grains. Use your hands. Then dry it out. I just leave it in a walk-in refrigerator for about an hour, sometimes overnight. Basically you want it as dry as you can get it without going through too much hassle.

5 **Dredge the rice with rice flour**, again separating it as much as possible. The more often you do this, the easier it becomes. Using a lot of rice flour helps. Fry it in small batches (the oil will want to overflow, so use a large pot) until golden-brown, and allow to dry on something covered with a lot of paper towels to catch the grease. You can crisp the rice an hour or two ahead of time, but after that window, it starts to harden and dry out again. It's worth making extra, because you'll want to snack on it.

6 **In a mixing bowl, toss the jellyfish well** with sugar, fish sauce, lime juice, and 1 T chili jam.

7 **Add the red onions, scallions, chilies, cilantro, and sawtooth**. Toss. Add 1 C crispy rice and peanuts, toss to coat. Add the ginger last. Divide among plates. Eat.

NAM TUK MAAENG GA PHROON

Jellyfish waterfall salad | Makes 2 servings

Steam sticky rice → **Blanch and grill jellyfish** → **Season jellyfish** → **Serve with sides**

While jellyfish generally isn't eaten in northern and northeastern Thailand, I figured I could prepare it in a way that's popular in both parts of the country—over a charcoal fire. *Nam tuk* translates as "waterfall," which, depending on whom you talk to, refers to either the sound of the meat grilling over charcoal, the fact that the juices of the sliced meat (usually beef or pork)

are incorporated into the dressing, or the fact that it's supposed to be spicy enough to make your eyes water. *Maaeng ga phroon* is jellyfish.

Texturally speaking, I had the best luck with salted jellyfish. I'm assuming that the end of the world will also wipe out any means of refrigeration, so salt-packing makes total sense. **—JOHNNY MONIS, LITTLE SEROW**

INGREDIENTS & EQUIPMENT

1 pound	salted jellyfish*, soaked in as many changes of water as you can manage
¼ C + 1 T	fish sauce
a pinch	sugar
¼ C	lime juice
3	small shallots, sliced
2 bunches	scallions, washed and thinly sliced
1 T or more	ground Thai chili powder
½ C	cilantro leaves and stems, roughly chopped
½ C	mint leaves
2 T	lemongrass, rough stuff removed, thinly sliced
2 T	uncooked sticky rice, toasted and ground
+	fresh herbs and vegetables (long beans, sliced cabbage, dill, quartered cucumbers)

STEAMED STICKY RICE

+	sticky rice

1 Prepare a charcoal grill. Quickly blanch soaked jellyfish in boiling water—just for a few seconds (it helps with the texture). Dry and toss with 1 T fish sauce and a pinch of sugar.

2 Make sure your grill grate is clean and well oiled. Grill the jellyfish, getting as much char on them as

For God's sake, soak salted jellyfish as many times as you can.

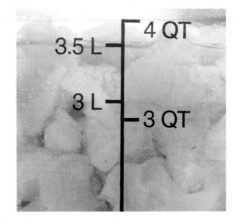

you can. Place on a cutting board and let the jellyfish rest for a few minutes before cutting into strips.

Some caveats:

1) Jellyfish shrink an incredible amount when grilled, so a cast-iron grill pan may be a better play, unless you're starting with really large pieces of jellyfish.

2) If this were a normal, desirable meat, filled with flavorful juices instead of corrosive salt water, I would note the fire should be raging hot and the grilling time as short as possible. This does not really apply to salted jellyfish. Just cook the pieces until they're charred. With other meats—like pork, which is what I usually use in this dish—adding the juices that run out of the just-charred meat to the dressing is an ace move. With the jellyfish, not so much.

3 Toss the grilled jellyfish with all the remaining ingredients (except the accompanying herbs and vegetables—long beans, cabbage, etc.) and place on one large plate. Serve with the other vegetables and baskets of sticky rice on the side.

* *A note from the editors on procuring salted jellyfish:* In these preapocalyptic times, fresh jellyfish can still be as hard to find as Santa Barbara spot prawns will be in the scorched hellscape of the future. Luckily, there's a place called Chinatown where any good-sized fishmarket should be able to help you out. In Manhattan's Chinatown, you can find salted jellyfish desalinating in tanks out in front of the fish display at Hong Kong Supermarket on Hester Street, much in the way one hears of baccalà being sold in whatever pastoral part of Italy it is where they sell a lot of salt cod.

The jellyfish was sold in three parts: tentacles, giant flaccid hoods, and "heads," which we assumed, with no rigorous research or real zoological understanding of the jellyfish, to be the thing that would be between the tentacles and the hoods if you were to put one of these things back together.

The heads were $9.99; the other parts were $2.99 and no part of it tasted any better or worse than the others. We soaked all of them in a few changes of water over the course of 24 hours before cooking them, and would advise you to do the same. Otherwise, foreswear this nasty fruit of the sea, even after the apocalypse.

STEAMED STICKY RICE

Scale this to make as much rice as you like.

1 Soak the rice in cold water for at least 3 hours. Drain and wrap in a double layer of cheesecloth. Steam in a covered steamer for 30 minutes. Cool briefly, then serve.

~~CHANTHABURI JELLYFISH~~

Cured Kingfish Salad | *Makes 1 serving*

Southeast of Bangkok, the province of Chanthaburi, which is pinned between the Gulf of Thailand and the Cambodian border, the cup jellyfish is caught in the morning and in brine by noon. Once the jellyfish is cleaned in salted water, it's then placed in a clay pot and mixed with splinters of the bark of a tree called copper shield. This bark imparts an eerie rosy hue to the beast. A little water is added and it's left to pickle for a few days.

And so it is sold in the markets there, usually just at the entrance, in buckets or ready-to-go plastic bags. I've only ever seen jellyfish sold in this province. It's eaten alone or with a chili and garlic sauce. It's mostly men who eat it, with a shot of whiskey to make it easier to swallow.

Something easier to prepare—and I think certainly easier to eat—is a simple dish of marinated kingfish. Let's make that instead. Even in the apocalypse, I think a slab of fatty, firm fish will be easier to get your hands on than the bark of an Asian ornamental tree and the bottle of whiskey you'll need to choke down some pickled jellyfish. You're prepared either way now. **—DAVID THOMPSON, NAHM**

INGREDIENTS	
3 oz	kingfish (amberjack or yellowtail) fillet, trimmed, bloodline removed
good pinch	salt
3 T	lime juice
3	shallots, sliced
2 stalks	lemongrass, trimmed and finely sliced
a handful	mint leaves
5	bird's eye chilies, halved, seeded, washed

1 **Slice the fillet in half lengthwise**, down the center, then slice it finely crosswise—one serving should be about eight slices. Combine the salt and lime juice in a bowl, add the fish, and mix well to marinate. Allow to stand for 3 to 4 minutes to cure. Combine with the remaining ingredients. It should taste sour, salty, and spicy. Adjust as necessary, and serve.

BOMB APPÉTIT!

BY ALEX WELLERSTEIN

One of the things that make nuclear weapons especially unpleasant is the fact that they have a nasty tendency to *contaminate.* Aside from causing slow, gruesome death from radiation poisoning, neutrons released in a nuclear explosion have the added bonus of rendering everything they touch radioactive.

During the early Cold War, when nuclear exchanges were a not-unlikely scenario, a serious question arose for the United States government.

In the event of nuclear war, what would happen to our lunch?

In theory, you could figure this sort of thing out in a lab: expose some food to radiation, see what happens. In reality, knowing how things would play out with an actual nuclear explosion is a complicated business to predict. And so, in 1955, the Federal Civil Defense Administration (the precursor to FEMA) arranged to have a diverse amount of food and beverages placed near two nuclear detonations, code-named

"Apple-1" and "Apple-2." The first "Apple" shot had an explosive force equivalent to 14,000 tons of TNT (approximately the same as the Hiroshima bomb), while the second's was 29,000 tons of TNT (about 50 percent more than the Nagasaki bomb).

The experiment, Project 32 of the larger Operation Teapot, encompassed an array of foodstuffs: apples, oranges, potatoes, onions, raisins, dehydrated milk, candy, frozen chicken pot pies, french fries, peas, Smithfield hams, bacon, sausages, beef rounds, legs of lamb, frankfurters, bologna, flour, crackers, prunes, macaroni, Jell-O.

On the whole, the food fared well. Even when stored out in the open in a big trench, most of the food wasn't heavily contaminated unless it

was within a quarter mile of the nuclear explosions. Even the items that did become problematically radioactive were rated as safe for "emergency use" after a few days. The food kept in freezers did fine, as long as the refrigeration equipment wasn't damaged: spoilage was more of a threat to the frozen meats than the bomb. There were a few exceptions: places where food and packaging intersected (grease spots from melted margarine and lard) became highly radioactive and stayed that way for a while. Potatoes exposed to nukes stopped sprouting.

Some of the foods exposed underwent chemical changes that affected their flavors. Rolled oats took on a "burnt metallic-type flavor" which, the scientists noted, "made it unacceptable by normal

standards." Dehydrated milk took on a "very strong stale flavor and odor when reconstituted." Frankfurters exposed to the bomb exhibited "quite startling" changes to appearance once reheated: "The constrictions, bulges, and curling apparent in these sausages were unique and quite different from any deformations ever observed in our laboratories before this." The hot dogs cooked by nuclear fire were reported to have an "undesirable" taste, described as "stale, rancid, cheesy, and metallic" by the team of taste-testers.

Another research program—Project 32.2a, "The Effect of Nuclear Explosions on Commercially Packaged Beverages"—was devoted to the question of whether beer and soft drinks would survive a nuclear holocaust. This question was especially important, the authors of the report explained, because "packaged beverages, both beer and soft drinks, are so ubiquitous and already uniformly available in urban

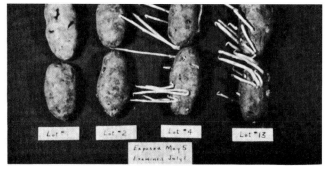

LEFT PAGE, TOP: Damaged soda and beer cans after a nuclear blast.

ABOVE: Photographs from the government reports on Project 32. *From top to bottom:* beer bottles to be exposed to a nuclear explosion; comparing the visual appearance of meat and meat products that were and were not exposed to a nuclear explosion a quarter mile away; hams recovered after the nuclear blast, located one mile from ground zero; potatoes at close distances to the nuclear explosion showed markedly inhibited sprouting (those on the left were a half mile or less from the blast).

areas, it is obvious that they could serve as important sources of fluids."

Fortunately, beer and soft drinks survived, relatively unscathed by nuclear explosion, at least by the radiation standards of the time. The only problem, the final report explained, was that they didn't taste very good:

"Representative samples of the various exposed packaged beers, as well as un-exposed control samples in both cans and bottles, were submitted to five qualified laboratories for carefully controlled taste-testing. The cumulative opinions on the various beers indicated a range from 'commercial quality' on through 'aged' and 'definitely off.' All agreed, however, that the beer could unquestionably be used as an emergency source of potable beverages. Obviously, if a large storage of such packaged beers was to be trapped in a zone of such intense radiation following a nuclear explosion, ultimate usage of the beverages beyond the emergency utility would likely be subject to review of the taste before return to commercial distribution."

These findings would most likely not apply in the present day. For one thing, Apple-1 and Apple-2 were tiny bombs,

even by the standards of the day. Today's nuclear weapons are hundreds of times more destructive. Modern beverage packaging is made of different materials than the cans of the 1950s. Aluminum, for example, is generally much more susceptible to radiation than tin. The tests also neglected the problem of fallout, the radioactive dust generated by mushroom clouds as they disperse. Nuclear fallout can work its way into the overall food supply, creating a long-term problem once stores have run out.

It's been a long time since the U.S. government has run live nuclear tests. Operation Teapot is a relic of another time, when the threat of nuclear warfare felt more imminent, yet more fantastical. Our fear of global nuclear warfare has since abated, but our familiarity with nuclear disaster—in the form of power-plant meltdowns—has unfortunately expanded. The tests in Operation Teapot were conducted in all seriousness; researchers fully expected that someday we'd all have to deal with the problem of a nuked lunch. Today, when considering nuclear fallout, it seems a bit too quaint to ask, "Will our beer be okay?" **LP**

FORING ~~FOR~~ WITH DUMMIES

Every decade or so foraging flares up as a food trend. High atop the bucket list of every food pervert is an afternoon spent crawling around in the dirt with René Redzepi; fifteen years before that it might have been Jean-Georges Vongerichten; a decade before him, Jean-Louis Palladin. Point is, at very fancy restaurants, chances are good that you've eaten something someone found.

But left to our own devices, how would we fare as scavengers in the postapocalyptic wasteland? We sent four relative know-nothings into the wild to collect what they thought—based on nothing but instinct—might be edible. Then we let bona fide foraging experts have a look. Their responses ranged from bemused ("I'm not sure about the wisdom of collecting a coral snake.") to not-so-bemused ("The number of poisonous plants is alarming.")

The experts couldn't identify everything, nor do they offer any guarantees about their IDs—it's hard to work from photos—but their guesses are certainly better than mine. **—CHRIS YING**

Additional thanks to: Kevin Feinstein, Iso Rabins, Daphne Richards

FLORIDA
Foraging by Jonathan Bremer & Carrie Guss
Identification by Green Deane, *eattheweeds.com*

Possibly **PEPPERVINE.** Generally considered inedible, if not toxic, because of high levels of calcium oxalate. If consumed in large quantities you could die without medical attention.

Could be the terminal cluster of a **SUMAC.** The tiny hairs on the berries can be used to make a vitamin-C rich drink. The berries can also be dried and ground into a spice. Additionally, in the spring, sumac shoots can be peeled and eaten raw or cooked. Avoid poison sumac. It has white berries and grows in damp places. Edible sumac has garnet-colored berries and grows in dry places.

The **GRAPEFRUIT** could be domestic or wild. If domestic, it's edible. Wild citrus is usually very acidic or bitter. The juice can be watered down and drunk, or the entire fruit mashed up and used as soap. Thorns on the branches can be used to make fish hooks.

BIDENS ALBA. Perhaps the best find. It can be eaten raw, but is far better boiled. It has twice the nutrition of spinach, and grows locally everywhere, all year long. Dried, it makes a tea that tastes nearly identical to green tea and has medicinal applications. The seeds can be dried then ground into a powder. That powder staunches blood flow and is a topical anesthetic. Juice from large leaves are good for a sore throat and the dried leaves make a good tobacco substitute.

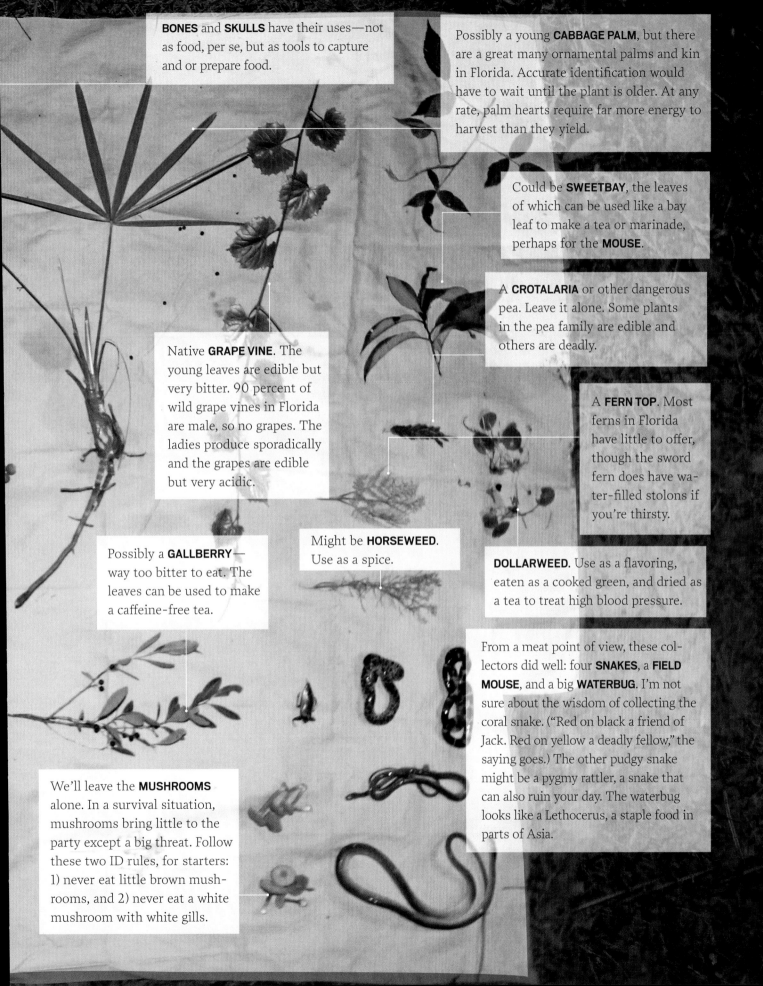

BONES and SKULLS have their uses—not as food, per se, but as tools to capture and or prepare food.

Possibly a young CABBAGE PALM, but there are a great many ornamental palms and kin in Florida. Accurate identification would have to wait until the plant is older. At any rate, palm hearts require far more energy to harvest than they yield.

Could be SWEETBAY, the leaves of which can be used like a bay leaf to make a tea or marinade, perhaps for the MOUSE.

A CROTALARIA or other dangerous pea. Leave it alone. Some plants in the pea family are edible and others are deadly.

Native GRAPE VINE. The young leaves are edible but very bitter. 90 percent of wild grape vines in Florida are male, so no grapes. The ladies produce sporadically and the grapes are edible but very acidic.

A FERN TOP. Most ferns in Florida have little to offer, though the sword fern does have water-filled stolons if you're thirsty.

Possibly a GALLBERRY— way too bitter to eat. The leaves can be used to make a caffeine-free tea.

Might be HORSEWEED. Use as a spice.

DOLLARWEED. Use as a flavoring, eaten as a cooked green, and dried as a tea to treat high blood pressure.

From a meat point of view, these collectors did well: four SNAKES, a FIELD MOUSE, and a big WATERBUG. I'm not sure about the wisdom of collecting the coral snake. ("Red on black a friend of Jack. Red on yellow a deadly fellow," the saying goes.) The other pudgy snake might be a pygmy rattler, a snake that can also ruin your day. The waterbug looks like a Lethocerus, a staple food in parts of Asia.

We'll leave the MUSHROOMS alone. In a survival situation, mushrooms bring little to the party except a big threat. Follow these two ID rules, for starters: 1) never eat little brown mushrooms, and 2) never eat a white mushroom with white gills.

OREGON

Foraging by Julia Raymond
Identification by John Kallas, PhD, *wildfoodadventures.com*

Most likely **SHASTA DAISY**, an ornamental whose young leaves and flowers are sometimes considered edible. But then again, there's a lot of misinformation out there.

Probably **CREEPING BUTTERCUP.** Mildly poisonous. Cattle eat it as a last resort when starving. Humans would probably get minor symptoms, like indigestion, diarrhea, possibly vomiting—a prescription for death in a true survival situation.

MUSHROOMS are not my expertise. And even though I think I know the one in the center, as a professional, it would be irresponsible for me to guess. When in doubt, do not eat. Mushrooms have no calories to contribute.

ROSE HIPS, probably different ornamental strains. These hips are not ripe yet. Once ripe, you can peel the hip off the seeds and eat them fresh, add them to salads, make fruit leather, jam them, make soup—anything you would do with a starchy, mildly sweet fruit. But too much unripe fruit may give you diarrhea.

COMMON HORSETAIL: There is really nothing to eat on this stringy fibrous plant. They are poisonous to livestock. Some health enthusiasts add tiny amounts of the young green parts to blended fruit drinks with no apparent ill effects. They have no flavor and no calories to speak of.

HARLEQUIN GLORYBOWER: An Asian ornamental tree that has a marvelous aroma when in flower. The young leaves and shoots can be edible if boiled, but there's not much information on the fruit's edibility.

These **LEAVES** by themselves are not enough to identify this plant.

MINNESOTA

Foraging by Christopher Sheehy
Identification by Sam Thayer, *foragersharvest.com*

BLACK RASPBERRY. This time of year, the leaves make a decent tea, but otherwise nothing edible until next growing season.

FOXTAIL MILLET. This grass has edible seeds, but the specimens here have dropped all their seed already. The time to get seeds is late summer.

CANADA THISTLE. The roots/rhizomes are edible, but only in spring and summer. Tender tips in summer, stems in late spring.

GRASS-LEAVED GOLDENROD. Makes an okay tea.

A **LICHEN** of some sort. Generally they are nontoxic but have little food value.

STINGING NETTLE. Good green (when cooked) from spring through fall, but best in spring. High in protein, more calories than the chickweed. Also makes a nice vegetable broth.

DANDELION. Edible green. The root is a better source of calories.

MOTHERWORT. A very bitter mint that is used medicinally and is definitely not a food plant. Dangerous if eaten in large quantities but it's so bitter that that's not usually a problem.

Unidentified **BARK.** If you're going to eat tree bark, you eat the inner bark, not this outer covering, which is essentially eating wood. Slippery elm's inner bark is a good survival food that is abundant in much of Minnesota.

WOOD SORREL. Edible, but really just a snack.

This may be **WILD CARROT.** If it is, the roots are small and slightly tough, but taste good and have some calories. But there are very poisonous plants that look similar to wild carrot. It is not actually hard to identify them, but you have to know how.

BUTTERCUP. Mildly toxic.

Some of this is **CHICKWEED**. Good leafy green from early spring through late fall. There appears to be a non-chickweed plant mixed in. This is a big red flag. It means the part of this person's brain that recognizes plants and categorizes them into types has been little used and isn't functioning to the capacity that would be biologically normal for humans.

A species of **ARTEMISIA**, probably common wormwood. None of them are food plants except possibly as tea.

This may be a perennial mustard such as **CARDAMINE**. Hard to tell. If it's cardamine, it's marginally edible (more of a horseradish-like seasoning).

MULLEIN. Not toxic, not a food plant either.

CATNIP. A mint with a similar texture to motherwort but different leaf shape. Catnip leaves are edible and can also be used for tea.

None of these **MUSHROOMS** look like toxic species, nor edible. They appear old, rotten, woody, and worthless.

PLANTAIN. Edible, but these leaves are tough and not going to provide much food value.

CROWN VETCH or a related vetch. Not edible and mildly poisonous.

TEXAS

Foraging by Ira Chute
Identification by Dr. Mark "Merriwether"
Vorderbruggen, *foragingtexas.com*

Looks a bit like **WILD ONION**. If it smells like onion/garlic, then it is edible and an excellent source of vitamin C. If it doesn't smell like an onion, don't eat it.

GRASS (specific type unknown). All grass seeds are edible, but to maximize nutritional value, they should be cooked in some way (boiled, roasted, toasted). The seeds offer some protein, which is vital, but difficult to harvest. The grass leaves themselves should be avoided as some can contain cyanide-type compounds.

PRICKLY PEAR. This is a classic Texas wild edible. Young, tender pads can be sliced up and then cooked like green beans. Older pads need to be skinned and have the thick veins within removed before cooking. They can also be seasoned and dehydrated into jerky.

Some sort of **BEETLE**. If it is a true beetle (six legs, wings, thorax, head) it is edible, but should be cooked first to kill any parasites. Once cooked, peel off the wings, pull off the head and legs, and eat the rest. It's protein.

ACORNS. These are edible once they've been shelled, crushed, and their tannic acid leached out with lots of running water. Once the tannic acid is removed acorns are an excellent source of protein, fats, and oil. The downside is that the oil in acorns goes rancid very quickly.

DANDELIONS. Filled with vitamins, minerals, and protein. They are, however, quite bitter. They're also a strong diuretic, so be ready to pee a lot if you eat a lot.

RIVERCANE. Young shoots can be used the same way as bamboo shoots. The stalks can also be used to make arrows, blowguns, frog-gigs, and many other useful things.

Could be **MESQUITE BEANS,** which can be pounded and boiled into a calorie-rich porridge. But if they're not mesquite beans, then they are most likely highly toxic. Sidenote: only use mesquite beans that have been picked directly from the tree. Once they fall and touch the ground they can be infected with a highly toxic fungus that causes madness and excruciating death.

It looks like **ROSEMARY.** If it smells like rosemary it is rosemary.

SILVER NIGHTSHADE. TOXIC! POISON! DEADLY! DO NOT EAT! However, 2–3 seeds crushed into a gallon of warm, raw milk will convert the milk to cheese. Silver nightshade seeds contain a natural, vegetable-based rennet enzyme which has been used to make cheese in Mexico for centuries.

JUNIPER BERRIES. These can be used in small quantities to season other foods. The needles can be used for a tea that some believe can help fight viral infections.

153

BUILDING SOMETHING OUT OF NOTHING

RECIPES FROM THE WASTELAND

Before we had the benefit of stoves and blenders and grocery stores, we still had cooking. Assuming a few enterprising members of our race survive the Great Fire/Freeze/Invasion/Server Crash, I imagine cooking will survive with them, too.

Professional cooks like to flaunt this fact. They brag often and loudly about how they will thrive in a postapocalyptic wasteland. Cooks have utility. They will survive. People always need to eat.

After pressing the issue a bit—*How would you even cook without your fancy kitchen? Do you remember how?*—I get the sense that they think about this stuff a lot.

Chad Robertson imagines a planet mobbed by murderous, dam-building rodents. Conveniently, the "werebeavers" stick to fresh water, so he's free to surf the oceans and collect kombu for his baking projects. Lee Tiernan's thoughts drift to the difficulty of wrangling a noncompliant cow into giving him milk for butter. Should the world descend into chaos, Daniel Patterson's plan involves ingratiating himself as personal chef to the warlord who presides over the production of sea salt.

For now, these remain the bleak fantasies of active imaginations. But should the world turn on its head, these guys will have a couple of recipes up their sleeves.

—CHRIS YING

THE SALT LORD'S PORK CHOP

From Daniel Patterson of Coi | *Makes 1 serving*

Evaporate sea salt → Brine pork chop → Cook potatoes → Grill pork chop → Make sauce; serve

You know what makes food taste good? Salt. You know what allows you to preserve food? Salt. You know what you can't live without? Salt. And you know what disappeared first from every store after the apocalypse? Beer, actually. And all the good tequilas. But after that? Salt.

There weren't many people left after it all went down, just the tough ones, smart ones, and lucky ones. A few were all three, and they saw the future in two things: water and salt. Some gangs hijacked the fresh water, and some took the salt. Between them they divided up the country.

There are two ways to get salt. There's land salt, which you dig out of the ground; and sea salt, which you dry from ocean water. The middle of the country trades in land salt. Land salt doesn't taste as good as sea salt, and the inland

Salt Lord is brutal; ask anyone who works in the mines. (Everyone works in the mines.) The coastal Salt Lord pretty much has it made: better salt, better land, and surfing.

I live on the coast. Though, there's not much coastal access now; it's mostly all used to make salt. They cordon off huge areas with walls to trap the seawater, then let it dry out. The good stuff is on top, white and flaky; then there's gray, coarse, minerally stuff underneath.

I'm one of the lucky ones. I only know how to do one thing, but it's pretty useful. Give me salt and some edible stuff and I can feed people. So I cook for the coastal Salt Lord. It's not a bad gig. He gives me run of the place—I can hunt boar, and harvest potatoes, herbs, and mussels. Plus, working for the Salt Lord means I can barter for other essentials: moonshine, 8-tracks... —**DANIEL PATTERSON**

INGREDIENTS & EQUIPMENT

3 qts	clean seawater
1	thick-cut pork or wild boar chop
2	waxy potatoes
1 T +	olive oil
1	shallot, sliced
1 clove	garlic, minced
10	mussels
¼ C	white wine
¼ C	water
½	lemon, juiced
+	grill and wood
+	herbs (fennel fronds, sea spinach) and flowers (radish, mustard, wood sorrel)

1 **Make sea salt**, either by letting 1 quart of seawater evaporate in a wide, shallow container, or by boiling it down. You'll get flakier stuff if you let the seawater evaporate, but it can take a while. Harvest the water from a clean source—far from sewage outlets and crowded beaches—and not after a recent rain.

Scrape the salt from the bottom of the vessel and store in a sealed container. Each quart of seawater should yield about 4 T salt. It's more than you need for this recipe, but remember, those who control the salt, control the world.

2 **Place the pork chop in 1 quart of seawater**, cover, and refrigerate (assuming you have access to refrigeration). Seawater has a slightly lower salt content than your typical brine, so let it marinate for 4–6 hours. If you don't have a fridge, let it brine at room temp for 2 hours.

3 **Let the pork chop sit in the seawater at room temperature** for about 1 hour before cooking. Start a fire or light some charcoal. Set up a grill once you've got embers going.

4 **Meanwhile, peel the potatoes** and place them in a small pot with 1 quart of seawater. Bring to a simmer over the fire, and cook the potatoes for about twenty minutes, or until tender. Seawater is exactly as salty as you want potato-cooking water to be. Once the potatoes are cooked, strain

and let them sit while you cook the pork. An interesting, tasty skin will form on the outside of the taters.

5 **Get the fire burning hot**. Pull the pork chop out of the brine and dry it as best you can. Place on the hot grill and cook for about 5 minutes on each side. The Salt Lord prefers his pork medium. If you've stolen a pig from a questionable camp of gypsies, cook the chop well. Let it rest while you make the sauce.

6 **Heat a small pot over the fire**, then add 1 tablespoon of olive oil. Toss in the shallot and garlic, and cook until fragrant. Add the mussels, white wine, and water. Cover and steam until the mussels open. Strain everything out, reserving the liquid. Feed the mussels to the lower caste. Season the sauce with olive oil, lemon juice, and fresh sea salt.

7 **The Salt Lord loves a well-composed plate**. Tear the potatoes apart and spread around the chop. Top with herbs and flowers, surround with sauce. Make a show of tasting the chop for poison before serving.

*1 quart of seawater should yield about 4 T salt (**step 1**).*

*Cook the pork over wood, charcoal, or now-useless paper currency (**step 3**).*

*You can eat the mussels, or discard them in a show of haughty indifference (**step 6**).*

BREAD

From Chad Robertson of Tartine Bakery | *Makes 10–12 servings*

| Find kombu | → | Sprout/grind flours | → | Build box and oven | → | Make dough | → | Bake; serve |

Long before the invasion, before the werebeavers took over, I started baking my own bread in a backyard oven in Northern California.

Things aren't much different now, to be honest. I bake, I try to be resourceful, I get by. If we steer clear of rivers, streams, and former urban areas, the beavers pretty much leave us alone. River mouths are tough. The graysuits—weresharks—still lurk in the ocean, and now we've got the beavers coming from the other side. (A full-grown werebeaver could take a gray on a good day.) So except for river mouths and days when the grays are on the prowl, I surf wherever and whenever I want. And when I'm out at the beach, I gather as much kombu kelp as I can.

The kombu's for baking. My current bread-baking style is a riff on the old East Coast clam or lobster bakes. I build a fire pit out of a load of bricks, light a fire and get everything searing hot, then line the interior with wet seaweed. I drop the bread in, cover with more seaweed, and find something big and flat to cover the pit. Then I let the whole thing steam-bake in the ground until the bread is done.

These days I don't always know where my grain is going to come from, or its baking qualities, so the technique needs to be forgiving. I also want to make sure the dough is well fermented, easily digestible, and fully cooked. The type of bread best suited to this sort of steam-baking is a Danish pumpernickel, a style I learned to make decades ago, when Scandinavia was the epicenter of the culinary universe. The bread dough is set into a thick wooden frame with a folded steel sheet on top and bottom to seal. It bakes overnight, insulated by seaweed. Wrapping the box in kombu ensures that the bread is baked in a steamy, sealed environment. All the glutamates from the kombu basically baste the bread as it cooks. Once baked, it keeps for a week or two, if properly wrapped.

This bread has a high percentage of whole-grain berries that don't really need to be ground into flour. Inspired by the wet-grinding tradition of corn masa in Mexico and Central America, and to make the whole thing more digestible, I soak and sprout the grains first. Rough grinding the moist, soft berries on a stone *matate* is easy after that. I also coarse-grind a small amount of dry wheat or rye berries into flour using a dry matate—this helps bind the dough into a workable mass. Plus I need some coarse flour for keeping the starter going with regular feedings.

As for the oven, it's a cinch. There are bricks all over the place. Look for the heaviest ones with good corners so you can build solid, leakproof oven walls. You can build a dry fire-pit oven with no mortar in less than an hour. If you have to move it quickly, the whole thing comes apart in the same amount of time. You'll want at least a day to fully saturate the bricks with heat, though.

Bread is elemental to those of us who remember the old days. People crave it, yearn for it. So I bake bread and the hungry masses leave me in peace. It's always been this way, really. I'm pretty much in the same situation I was before the apocalypse, though nobody lines up for the bread anymore. I have it ready in the afternoon. People expect it from me. But if it's not ready by dinnertime, I've got serious trouble.

INGREDIENTS & EQUIPMENT	
1050 g	sprouted rye berries
1 kg	coarse whole grain flour (wheat or rye)
850 g	water

620 g	levain
90 g	sunflower seeds
41 g	brown flaxseeds
360 g	whey or sour milk
270 g	beer

32 g	salt
+	kombu
LEVAIN	
+	whole-grain flour
+	water

photos by Chad Robertson

1 Forage kombu for insulating the bread.

2 To sprout rye berries, I soak them for 4–6 hours in cold water, drain thoroughly, and cover with cloth. Kept in a moderately warm place and rinsed thoroughly twice a day (morning and night), the grain should sprout in 2 or 3 days. Using a *metate* (flat stone mortar), coarsely grind the sprouts.

    Grind dry wheat into flour using the same metate. Push the stone dowel along the grinding surface using your weight to crush the grains. Keep a layer of grains between the dowel and surface, otherwise you'll add rock dust to your dough. Set something under the metate to catch loose grains

and add them back in the mix. The texture you want is a mix of powdery flour and cracked bits of grain.

3 My friend built me this 14"×7"×5" bread box out of beech wood. Beech is the traditional wood used for bread boxes like this in Scandinavia—it's very dense and tightly grained.

4 Create a simple fire pit by stacking found bricks. The pit should be big enough to leave about 6" of space around the bread box. You could make it bigger if you want to bake multiple loaves, small animals, the occasional werebeaver tail, etc. Dry out the fire pit completely. I do a couple of preliminary burns to make sure the bricks are completely dry.

5 To mix the dough, combine the water and levain* in a bucket. Add the coarse flour, seeds, and other liquids and mix slowly by hand until combined thoroughly. Let the dough rest, covered, for half an hour. Add salt and mix for another 10–12 minutes, then slowly add the crushed sprouted berries and mix to incorporate.

6 Cover the dough and let it rise at warm room temperature for 2–3 hours, turning it occasionally. Dip your hands in water and scoop the dough into the box. Smooth the top of the loaf with wet hands. Let it rise for 2 hours at warm room temperature, then overnight in a cool place.

7 On bake day, I burn wood for 8 hours to get a 4" bed of coals.

8 When you're ready to bake, score or dock the loaf on top, and brush with water. Set a grate over the coals, then kombu, then the box. Wrap in more seaweed. I bake the bread overnight—covered with a sheet tray and a piece of plywood to insulate.

9 and **10** Let the bread cool for at least half a day before cutting into it. This bread keeps well for up to a week.

■ To make levain: mix whole-grain flour and water to make a paste. Covered and kept in a moderately warm place, it will begin to ferment after a couple days. Discard half and refresh with more flour and water. Repeat twice daily until it smells sweet like yogurt and floats when you drop a bit into liquid.

BUTTER

From Lee Tiernan of St. John Bread & Wine | *Makes about 5 tablespoons*

Separate cream	→	Agitate

Making butter is pretty straightforward. Milk a cow, separate the cream, agitate it, and you're done. After the apocalypse, obtaining enough milk will be the biggest hurdle in the process, especially if you're looking to milk a wild cow for the first time. (You can watch wild-cow milking contests online, if you want to get a sense of the difficulty level.) A few precautions may save your life. Don't try to milk a bull. If you've mistakenly approached and angered a bull, pray that you have the time to cut your losses and find some olives to press for oil instead. Females with young calves can be just as aggressive and unapproachable, so caution should be exercised there, too.

Once you've identified an animal that looks like she might be amenable to being milked, you'll need to build up trust with the animal. Talk softly to her, and stay in the cow's line of sight. Cows respect confidence but not aggression. Once you have successfully gained the bovine's respect, you may find yourself with the privilege of milking her.

Pat and rub the udders to "bring the milk down," a term and method farmers use to relax the cow, mimicking a calf butting the udder with its nose when it wants to feed. Sit on a stool or bucket, not the ground, so you can move quickly if the cow grows angry. Cows spook easily, especially ones that haven't been milked before. Don't be surprised if the cow shits or pees or both. If you see her tail rising, move yourself and your milk-harvesting vessel out of splattering distance. Don't flip out or you run the risk of scaring her off.

Clamp the middle of the teat between your thumb and index finger, palm down. Gently squeeze the teat, the milk should flow in a nice, straight jet. Relax your grip and repeat until the udder is exhausted and the teat looks spent. The milk may be a little slow to flow at first, but will free up after a few squeezes. A liter of whole milk will contain between 3 and 5 percent butterfat, so you'll need a fair amount of milk to get a decent knob of butter. Good luck with that.

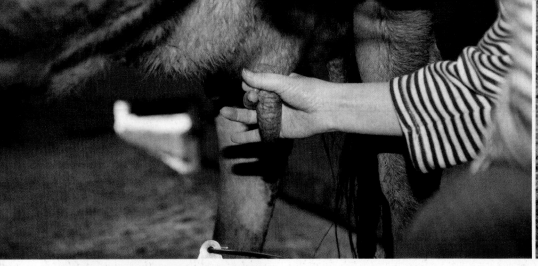

INGREDIENTS & EQUIPMENT

1 gal	raw milk
+	appropriate vessel
+	salt

1 **Refrigerate fresh milk** for 12–36 hours, allowing the fat to rise to the top. This process will also

the fat will rise to the surface, ready to be skimmed.

b. Deep-Setting Method: This method is a little quicker and slightly more effective. Pour the milk into a deep, narrow container. Leave somewhere cool for 24 hours. (Don't let the cream freeze; it screws with the fat globules). Ideally, this would take place in a sterilized glass cylinder

uid. When the time comes, use a pin to prick the end and release the milk.

2 **Place the skimmed cream** into a container—double the volume of cream—with a tight-fitting lid. Shake the container. The idea is to agitate the cream until it separates into a liquid (buttermilk) and fat (butter). It helps if the container is clear

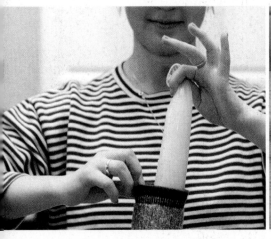

allow raw milk to culture, encouraging aroma and acidity, and improving the final product.

If you don't have access to a fridge, secure the container in a slow running stream. As for how to store the milk, there are two methods:

a. Shallow-Pan Method: Pour the milk into a flat tray, and store it in a cool place. After thirty-odd hours,

with a convenient tap at the bottom for easy milk straining. You can improvise with a clear, clean plastic bottle that can be pierced easily to release the liquid. If the milk is chilled well, the cream will solidify and remain in the container as the milk runs out. A non-lubricated condom will also suffice. They're easy to carry around and hold up to one liter of liq-

so you can see what's happening inside. Depending on how enthusiastic your shaking is, you should see some results after ten minutes. Once you've got a fair amount of butter built up, strain the buttermilk and reserve. It's tasty and a good accompaniment to the butter. Add a pinch of salt to the butter, and knead it in gently. Eat, or trade for supplies.

photos by Alanna Hale

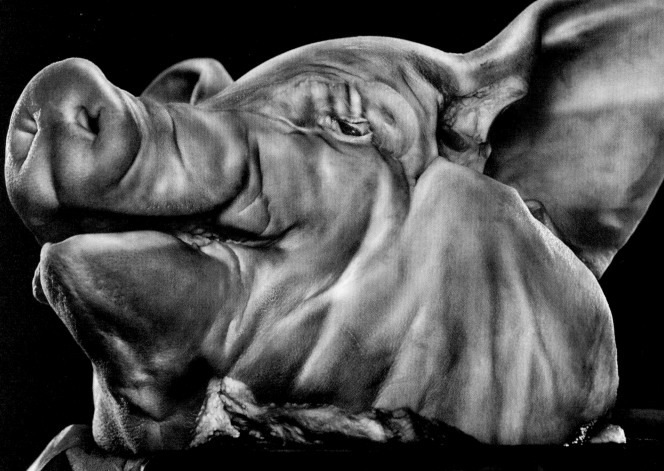

Last Supper

by **CHRIS ADRIAN** and **JOHN CROWLEY**

photographs by **JILL GREENBERG**

Dear John,

Are you on Twitter? Are you interested in the Pope? Do you remember me? Do you like unusual meats and cheeses? Do you like good wine and handsome people in costumes? Do you like orgies *of the intellect*?

If you answered *Yes* to any of these questions, you should come to a dinner my mother is calling her Last Supper, in honor of the Pope and his Last Tweets of the Apocalypse. It would be impossible to relay how big a fan you have in Mother, but permit me to make clear how much it would mean to her—in fact to all of us, the whole family—if you should be able to join us for this very special meal. This letter is your invitation—just present it at the door. I've enclosed a photograph of a dish we're planning: *Sighing Pigg* (Tweet Number 171). Don't worry, it's totally vegetarian!

All best,
Chris Adrian

P.S. February the Fifteenth, 2013, at Seven o'Clock at One and One Half Commercial Street, Provincetown, MA 02657

My dear Chris—

Good to hear from you after such a long silence. Thank you for this invitation, which I find, however, impossible to accept. Once I was invited to a performance-art event at which a crazed female, after feeding us a rich if slovenly banquet, unveiled a final bit of ugly meat we were each to have nibble of. What was it? She wouldn't say, but because of legal and moral complications we were to swear silence. Spewing and riot ensued. Of course it was just a *performance—food as art*—but still I feel that morsel in my gut. You can see why I cannot easily sit down before *something that purports to be pig but is not.*

Apologies to your mother—
John Crowley

Dear John,

How can I change your mind? Yours is the only invitation I've been trusted with and it seems I'm doing a terrible job of it. I ought to have explained more.

You're aware, aren't you, of the great furor in the whole enormous Body of Catholicism on account of the WikiLeak of the third Secret of Fatima, and the great surprise elicited by Pope Benedict when, instead of denying that the letter contained a date-specific warning about the end of the world, he embraced the warning and the date as real and took to Twitter to describe the nature of the coming Apocalypse and to call for a very hurried and last-minute housecleaning of the individual and collective Catholic soul? Like my mother, I suspect that your reaction to these developments is a highly nuanced combination of fascination and despair. Not personal despair—no, I can tell from reading your books that you're not a quitter like that old Pope—but Despair for the People, for the Body Catholic and that portion of

Twitter and the World that is leaping enthusiastically into the Pope's Apocalypse Hole. Like my mother, you would like to do something on that day to demonstrate your solidarity with Hope and Art, with Humanism and Humanity. Such will be this feast. You needn't be afraid.

Hopefully,
C.

P.S. IT WILL ALL BE DELICIOUS. Enclosed, another dish Mother has planned: *Bloody Kisses.*Not chicken, but not, despite appearances, lamb either, and a play of course on Tweet #232: *And in these days the lamb will give Bloody Kisses to the Faithful, so they will know themselves and know each other.*

Chris—

An apocalypse is not an *ending* at all, but an *opening*, which is more like a beginning, even if it's the beginning of the end. The opening of a book, a scroll, or—I've somehow always imagined it—a menu: one of those huge many-leaved red-sateen tasseled things you are handed in old-fashioned French restaurants and open in a mix of anticipation and the expectation of disappointment (What, no *tripes à la mode de Caen*? And they call this place French?).

It would be wrong to say I am *afraid.* I am a *good sport*. But your photographs—the "pigg," the "bloody kisses" (which looks to be a llama, I think, not a lamb)—part of your high spirits here in the face of apocalypse, I suppose—a universal Fool's Feast where everything forbidden is compulsory—or whatever the phrase is—I have to leave them facedown on my bedside table. Anyway—if your feast is real I will come.

JC

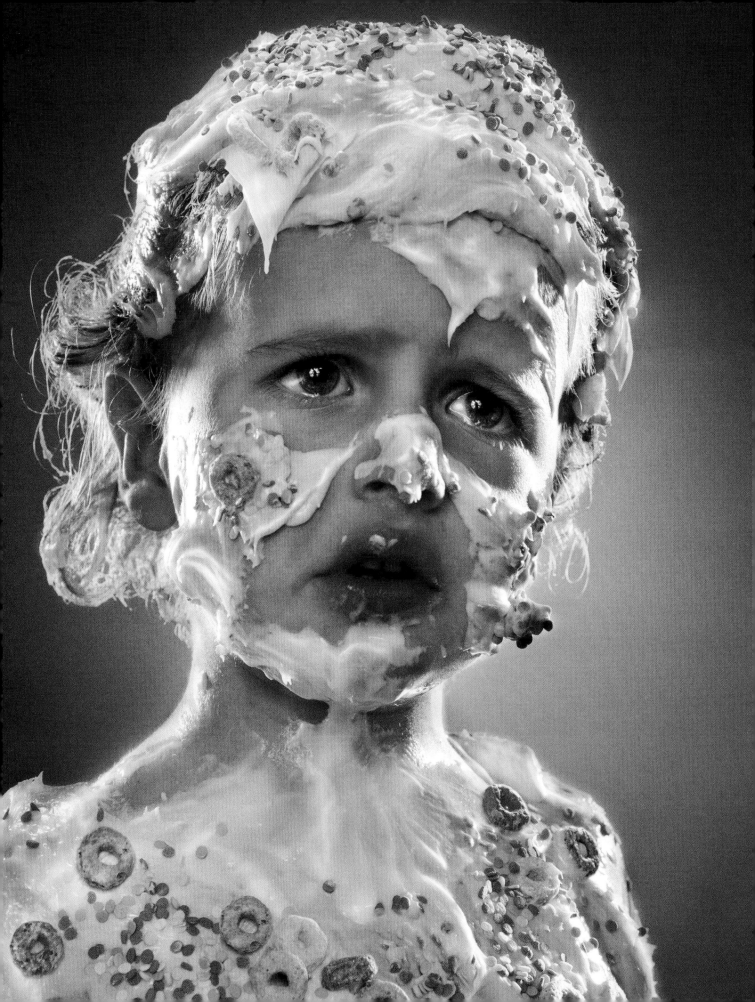

Dear John,

I shared your response with Mother, who ran around the whole house waving it and shouting, "Exactly! Exactly!" She then read aloud that bit about the menu and did that thing where you sort of eat your fingers and then make like you're scattering seed to pigeons and say, *Mwah!* You know? Like Chef Boyardee when he is really pleased with his sauce.

We are not delighted with the Pope. We are trying, as Mother says, to *do something about him*. We are trying to offer some imaginative counterbalance to his mad dark Tweets, to shape the world to come after a better image than bloody-mouthed lambs. The Pope wants the world to end, but we want it to begin! If His Holiness is on to something, and even if he is not, what better way to honor the best angel of his intentions than by sitting down in sincere fellowship and bending our hearts and imaginations toward that sort of Opening while the Pope sits in his closet gnawing his fingers and listening to Tool? I'll seem a Pollyanna if I say we'll open that Menu together and order Hope instead of Madness, but I don't care. Mother says I have my sincerity from my father, whoever he is, and today, in the context of this ongoing invitation, I'm not ashamed of it. Not at all.

But hooray, if I have understood you correctly! You sort of slipped it in at the end, but that looked like *Yes I'll come*. You know the way to Provincetown? Just get on Route 6 and drive until it ends. You'll see the Woods Hole light-house off to your right across the harbor, and there, on the hill to your left, is the house (it's an unmistakable Walter Gropius). Just drive on up and ring the bell. I will greet you or send Queenie, the butler. Hooray!

C.

Chris—

Here I am! So sorry you (or Mother) couldn't be here to greet me. As Kurt Vonnegut once remarked, if ever you tell a writer, "I like your work" be prepared to have him show up at your door soon after with a six-pack, ready to hear more. Or, in my case, a bottle of 1982 Château Mouton Rothschild, all that was of interest in the wine shop I stopped at on the dark road upward to this place. "Cigar box," said the salesman, "dark and with a tiny dagger of mint, a little scary but powerful." May it open hearts and mouths. Queenie, your "man," as they say in old novels about the upper crust (does every thought somehow lead to food here?), was the soul of suave humility. I didn't get the getup, but I'm sure jollity awaits. Oh, but I must ask—that child—there in the bath—I opened that door in error—what had befallen her? I know very well what little girls are made of—but shouldn't it all—the sugar and spice—stay inside?

The mitre and cope actually fit. I have not used the chrism, which looks nasty. My own favorite was Pius IX, Pio Nono—who invented Infallibility, the curse of every Sanctissimus since, including the new guy. Pio Nono! Pio Nono! I am ready for dinner.

JC

Dear John,

First of all, of course they fit! Second: welcome! Queenie brought me your note. So sorry I wasn't there to greet you as promised. Sorry, also, for all the mystery, the brightly lit but very quiet house, and no human faces to greet you but Queenie in that wrestling mask he likes to wear. Sorry for the will-o'-the-wisp lights that led you down to dinner, for the table so full of food and so empty of people, and sorry, finally, for this note on your plate.

I'm so glad you've come, and so sorry to have deceived you. The idea of my mother is in fact just an idea, though I have lived with her here for years. It's all true, in its way, what I wrote—how it is necessary for someone to sit at this table to feast and dream, but it isn't exactly a party. Yes Gourmands. Yes Apocalypse. But the Pope is just another man who's said yes to despair. Does his pain, and do his Tweets matter any more than the Tweets and the pain of the other 500 million users? No, they do not. And isn't that where the Apocalypse actually comes from, not out of the cave at Fatima and not at the end of time, but here right in the middle of it, every night, out of millions and millions of breaking hearts? And every morning a dawning world to come that could be Hell but is always a little better than that. Everyone is talking about 2013 as the year we finally say goodbye to Apocalypse, the year we all start reading children's books about Proust instead, but what they really mean is that we'll forget about it for a while. It's too much for everyone to think about all the time, and too hard for almost everyone to think about *in the right way*, and by that I mean, as you say, as a *beginning*, as a *menu*, an *opening*. Hence this house, full of all sorts of horrors and delights. (You'll have time to explore. Just don't waste your time looking for an exit. The doors all lead inside!) Hence this table, this feast.

Chris for God's sake where are you? What has become of the butler? All I have to write on is your note here. I don't think this is the bottle I brought. I haven't bathed. Does that matter? I have been brave. I was at last ready. I really believe that. But. Perhaps I never mentioned a serious murmur of the heart, aortic stenosis technically, unwell, I think actually I must now

Oh, I wish I had more time and room to explain, but I really am constrained. I won't tell you who my predecessor was here (would you believe it was Orson Scott Card, brilliant writer of Mormon Pornography?), but he didn't do a very good job of telling me what was going on. There was only the fan letter, and my arrival, and the empty house. But I figured it out soon enough. Somebody somewhere in the world has got to eat their heart out every day and nonetheless every night dream of beauty and justice—and now, for a little while, that person is you. And maybe you'll say *I do that anyway*—you are a writer after all, and a maker of masterpieces. But for a little while you'll have to do it here and in this way.

No no I don't think your mother understood I am an ordinary writer None of it was meant to be taken seriously A second read will prove it It does no one any good or any harm Please

And I do mean a little while. I promise to come back, and if I don't manage to, I have every faith that you'll be able to bring someone else here the way we were both brought. No one should have to do this, but you'll probably agree that somebody ought to. I'll send a note to your family, to keep them from worrying too much. Now I'm out of room, and time—the door you've opened for me is closing!

The children are here. Is that a llama? I SEE HER NOW SHE'S

Gratefully! Admiringly!
Chris Adrian

P.S. My own heart is empty of irony but full of gratitude and love when I tell you...*Bon Appétit!* Ⓛ

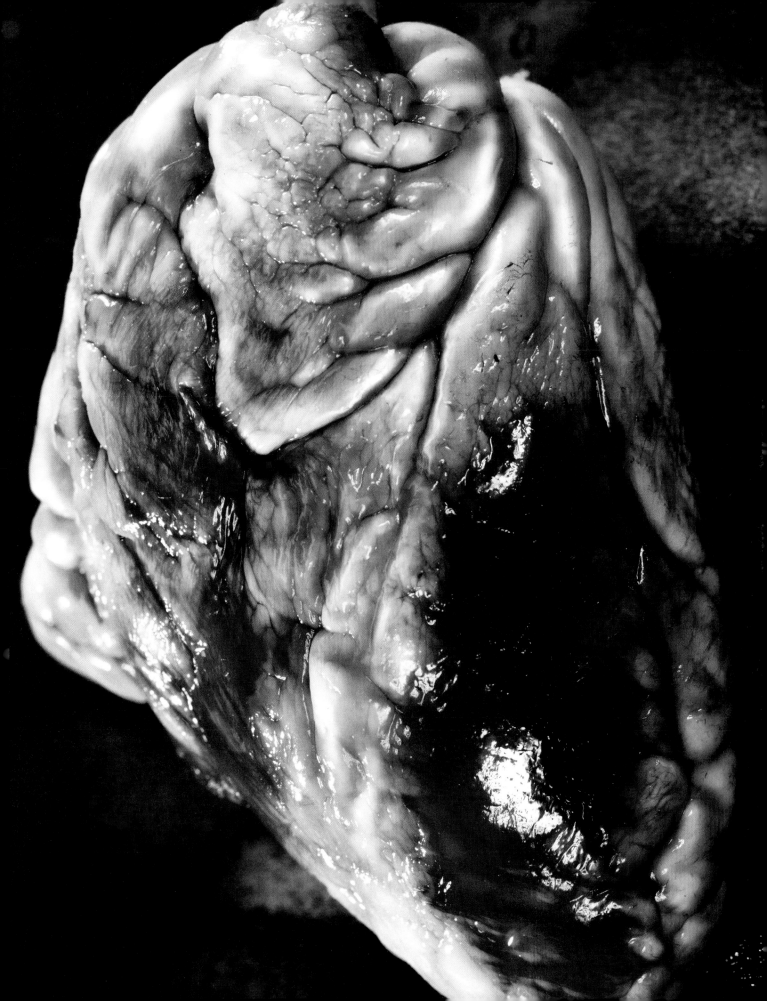

CONTRIBUTORS

CHRIS ADRIAN is the author of three novels and a collection of short stories, and has held fellowships from the NEA and the John Simon Guggenheim Memorial Foundation. He lives in Brooklyn, where he's training to become a hospital chaplain and working on a collection of short stories about American Puritans. John Crowley's *Aegypt* is pretty much his favorite novel ever.

NINA BAI is a science writer in Brooklyn, NY. Astrologically, she is a Capricorn and the tail of a Rat.

ALBERTO CÁCERES is a photographer based in the Yucatán.

JOSH COCHRAN grew up in Taiwan and the United States. He graduated with honors from Art Center College of Design and started working as an illustrator immediately after school. His work is commissioned by a diverse group of clients in editorial, advertising, publishing, broadcast, and the web. Josh also teaches at the School of Visual Arts and occasionally fills in art directing for the *New York Times* op-ed page. Josh lives in Brooklyn with his small dog Porkchop.

BILL COTTER lives in Austin with the poet Annie La Ganga. His second novel, *The Bearing Wall*, is due out in early 2014.

JOHN CROWLEY is the author of thirteen novels and several volumes of short fiction. Winner of a World Fantasy Lifetime Achievement award, an Award in Literature of the American Academy and Institute of Arts and Letters, the Premio Flaiano (Italy), his books have been translated into a dozen languages. He teaches creative writing at Yale. A recent favorite novel was Chris Adrian's *The Great Night*.

SARA CWYNAR is an artist and a graphic designer at the *New York Times Magazine*. Cwynar is represented by Cooper Cole Gallery in Toronto and has shown her work at the Museum of Modern Art and Printed Matter in New York. She is one of *Print Magazine*'s 20 Under 30 New Visual Artists and an ADC Young Gun. She makes photographs, installations, and books.

DARK IGLOO is a company that specializes. To see more of their photography, illustration, and video work check out *darkigloo.com*.

JAMIE FELDMAR is a Brooklyn-based journalist with a firm conviction in the power of an unlimited MetroCard. She has written for *Saveur*, the *Paris Review*, and the *Art of Eating*, among others. Visit her at *jamiefeldmar.com*.

ALEX FORBES was trained to become a food writer from a young age. Today she's a columnist at *Folha de São Paulo* newspaper and the food editor at *GQ Brazil*, besides contributing to several North American publications.

Since the age of ten, **JILL GREENBERG** has staged photographs and created characters using the mediums of drawing, painting, sculpture, film, and photography. She is known worldwide for her uniquely human animal portraits which intentionally anthropomorphize her subjects, as well as her infamous series, "End Times."

ALANNA HALE is a photographer, writer, and generally food-obsessed individual living in San Francisco with one very handsome man and one very handsome English bulldog. She'd probably be delighted if you took a look at some of her work up at *alannahale.com*.

BETH HOECKEL is an artist from Baltimore, MD. She creates collages from vintage publications, mixed media paintings, drawings, and beyond. See it all at *bethhoeckel.com*.

SANDOR ELLIX KATZ is a self-taught fermentation experimentalist. His books *The Art of Fermentation* and *Wild Fermentation*, and the fermentation workshops he has taught across North America and beyond have helped to catalyze a broad revival of the fermentation arts. For more information, check out his website *wildfermentation.com*.

LLOYD KAHN is the founding editor-in-chief of Shelter Publications, Inc. He is also an author, photographer, and pioneer of the green building and green architecture movements. He's on the web at *lloydkahn-ongoing.blogspot.com*.

AMANDA KLUDT is the editorial director of *Eater.com*. She lives in Brooklyn with a hairy drummer.

GENEVIEVE KO is a graduate of Yale University. She is a freelance food writer and a consultant to chefs and restaurants. She lives in New York City.

TIM LANE is a freelance illustrator and graphic novelist. His next graphic novel, *Folktales*, is expected to be published in spring, 2014.

SARAH LASKOW lives in New York City and has written about the environment for *Good*, the *American Prospect,* the *New Republic*, and other publications.

MARISSA LOUISE lives in Portland where she is part of the Noirwal Illustration Collective. Her illustrations have been featured in the *Willamette Weekly* and *Bear Deluxe Magazine*.

MARY MATSON & **MATT EVEN** are designers, chocolate makers, and art lovers living in Brooklyn. They met in high school and have been collaborating ever since.

HAROLD McGEE writes about the science of food and cooking. He's the author of *On Food & Cooking: The Science & Lore of the Kitchen*, *Keys to Good Cooking*, and posts at *curiouscook.com*.

TONY MILLIONAIRE was born in Boston and grew up in Gloucester, Massachusetts. He writes and draws the ongoing adventures of Sock Monkey, published by Dark Horse Comics. He is the creator of the syndicated comic strip, *MAAKIES*, which has been collected by Fantagraphics, who also publishes his graphic novel series, *Billy Hazelnuts*, and his latest book *500 Portraits*. His house is infested with kids, pets, toys, and a beautiful wife.

LINDSAY MOUND is an illustrator and musician working in Brooklyn. Her work, and links to her extracurricular blog and music, can be found on *lindsaymound.com*.

ROBYN O'NEIL was born in Omaha, Nebraska, and currently lives in Los Angeles. Her work was included in the 2004 Whitney Biennial. She is the recipient of numerous grants and awards, including an Irish Film Board grant. *robynoneil.com*.

MICHAEL POLLAN is the author of *Food Rules*, *In Defense of Food*, *The Omnivore's Dilemma*, and *The Botany of Desire*, all *New York Times* bestsellers. A longtime contributor to the *New York Times*, he is also the Knight Professor of Journalism at Berkeley. His new book, *Cooked: A Natural History of Transformation*, will be released in Spring 2013.

AMY JEAN PORTER has drawn more than 1,200 species of animals for her ongoing project "All Species, All the Time." Many of them can be found at *amyjeanporter.com*.

LOREN PURCELL is an Oakland, CA–based designer and illustrator. After relocating to the Bay Area in 2002, he graduated from the California College of the Arts to pursue his pre-teen dream of designing skateboard graphics for a living.

RON REGÉ, JR.'s new esoteric comics textbook *The Cartoon Utopia*, out now from Fantagraphics, is inspired by various alchemical and new thought texts as well as Maja D'Aoust's "Magic Class" lectures in LA, where Regé lives and performs in the band Lavender Diamond. Their new album *Incorruptible Heart* is out now from Paracadute.

GABRIELE STABILE is a photographer who lives with his family in downtown Manhattan.

JOHN JEREMIAH SULLIVAN is a contributing writer to the *New York Times Magazine* and the author most recently of *Pulphead: Essays*. He lives in Wilmington, North Carolina, with his wife and daughters.

SCOTT TEPLIN, an artist living and working in New York City, sometimes wishes he could just take a healthy food pill instead of eating real food. That's not to say he doesn't appreciate good food—it's just that sometimes he'd rather draw than cook, reheat, or go out to a restaurant and interact with others.

GABE ULLA is the features editor of *Eater.com*. He lives in New York City. He had a hard time writing in the third person.

CHRIS VON SZOMBATHY is a visual/audio artist/designer and art director from Vancouver, Canada. His work has been seen in everything from the small print to the big screen. He is unusually and excessively fond of ginger. *chrisvonszombathy.com*.

JOY Y. WANG is a producer for WNYC and has written for the *New York Times*, the *Wall Street Journal*, and *Newsweek*. She's originally from Knoxville, Tennessee, but is now just another journalist living in Brooklyn.

JOHN WARNER is the author of the novel, *The Funny Man*. He lives and eats in Charleston, SC.

JING WEI is an illustrator and printmaker based in Brooklyn.

ALEX WELLERSTEIN is an historian of nuclear weapons at the American Institute of Physics. His blog, Restricted Data, is at *nuclearsecrecy.com*.

ANNE WHEELER lives and writes and eats (a lot) in New Orleans. She also writes a column about atomic tourism for *McSweeney's*.

PAUL WINDLE currently lives and works in Brooklyn. He has worked with the *New York Times*, *Bloomberg BusinessWeek*, and others. Paul has recently been featured in American Illustration 31 and awarded the Art Directors Club Young Guns X award.

JAMI WITEK lives in San Francisco with her fiancé Chris and dog Huck.

BENJAMIN WOLFE is a culinary mycologist at Harvard, studying cheese, fermented meats, and other perfectly rotten foods. He is working on a book about mold. His husband, **SCOTT JONES**, a sous chef at No. 9 Park in Boston, finds rotten food hidden all over their house. Their cat, Higginsdale Fitzgerald Wolfe-Jones, is disgusted by it. *@LupoLabs*

LAURIE WOOLEVER is a contributing editor at *Wine Spectator* and a former executive editor at *Art Culinaire*, who's just waiting for *Lucky Peach* to give *Showgirls* the *Road House* treatment.

KRIS YENBAMROONG is the chef and owner of NIGHT+MARKET, a Thai restaurant in LA. Find him on Twitter: *@NtMRKT*.

JOOHEE YOON is an illustrator/printmaker based on the East Coast. She likes to draw almost as much as she likes to cook.

ALLEN YUEN is the general manager at Mission Chinese Food New York. He's online at *allenyuen.com*.